# A SUSSEX GUIDE

# 20 SUSSEX GARDENS

LORRAINE HARRISON

*Illustrated by*
SARAH YOUNG

SNAKE RIVER PRESS

# SNAKE RIVER PRESS

**Book No 3**
*Books about Sussex for the enthusiast*

Published in 2015 by
SNAKE RIVER PRESS
South Downs Way, Alfriston, Sussex BN26 5XW
**www.snakeriverpress.co.uk**

ISBN 978-1-906022-02-0

This book was conceived, designed and produced by
SNAKE RIVER PRESS

ART DIRECTOR & PUBLISHER *Peter Bridgewater*
EDITORIAL DIRECTOR *Viv Croot*
EDITOR *Robert Yarham*
PAGE MAKEUP *Richard Constable & Chris Morris*
ILLUSTRATOR *Sarah Young*

This book is typeset in Perpetua & Gill Sans,
two fonts designed by Eric Gill

Printed and bound in Poland

———

## DEDICATION

*For my very special mother, Blanche Harrison*

# CONTENTS

# INTRODUCTION

*'God Almighty first planted a garden; and, indeed,
it is the purest of human pleasures'.*

**FRANCIS BACON** *(1561-1626)*

Sussex is a blessed county. That loveliest combination of pretty towns and villages set within a varied landscape of countryside and coastline makes it one of the most attractive of the southern counties of England. For those who are lucky enough to live here, or to visit, and are interested in gardens then Sussex has even greater attractions. The favoured climate is kind to gardens (and to gardeners) and can accommodate a wide variety of plants both native and from far flung habitats. The county is large and wide, comprising both East and West Sussex and varies considerably in soil and shelter. Little surprise then to find that over the centuries some wonderful gardens have been made on Sussex chalk and clay and indeed continue to be made with enthusiasm today.

Much of my own time over the last ten years has been happily spent turning a patch of Sussex downland into a new garden. High on top of the Downs, with salt-laden winds and ground that when turned with a spade yields more flints and chalk than soil, my garden now flourishes. It has been an education visiting the gardens of Sussex – some share my conditions and successfully grow all the plants that love the dry alkaline soil, others produce the tremendous blousy blooms of the acid-loving azaleas and rhododendrons – all are a tribute to their makers and those who work so hard to make such beautiful spaces available for us to enjoy. Gardens offer so much; they are places of solace, inspiration, work, stimulation, leisure and contemplation. You need never have so much as lifted a trowel to enjoy their treasures and I hope all will find something fulfilling in each of my chosen Edens.

## An embarrassment of riches

Such a wealth of beautiful gardens has made choosing just 20 a very difficult task. Some of the guidelines I have employed to help structure the choice include a good geographical, historical and stylistic spread along with access for visitors over a long season. I have also tried to include a wide variety of sites, from the very old to the very new, from the large and grand to the small and domestic and from the privately owned to the municipally managed. The maintenance and access to each type of garden presents its own particular challenges, problems and advantages and will, I hope, add considerable variety and interest to the visitor's experience.

Doubtless a glimpse at the contents page and my list of chosen gardens will elicit cries of 'But where's Wakehurst Place?', 'How could she leave out Sheffield Park?' and 'Why did she choose This Garden but not That One?' I am the first to admit that Sussex is in the fortunate position of having something of an embarrassment of riches in the department of important and spectacular gardens. Certainly both Sheffield Park and Wakehurst Place are gardens of the first rank and I urge anyone inter-ested in gardens to visit both. However, part of the aim of this guide is to show the range and scope of gardens available to visitors across the whole county and also to highlight some of those that do not receive quite so much publicity. That being said, all the gardens featured here are long-time favourites of mine and one of the great pleasures of writing this book has been the revisiting of so many 'old friends.' I hope those who feel I have committed the sin of omitting their favourite garden will find some recompense in the Other Gardens to Visit section to the rear of this book. If not, please forgive me.

Gardens are not just about plants but are also about people, there-fore some gardens have been included not simply because they are lovely (although all are!) but also because they are intrinsically linked to the people who made them. Without some knowledge of the lives of Rudyard Kipling or Vanessa Bell a visit to Bateman's or to Charleston Farmhouse would, I feel, be a lesser experience. The antiquity of the house, land and garden at Bateman's provided Kipling with roots in a mother country in which he had lived so little of his life. Charleston was initially a retreat for Bell, her children and her lover, while the artist's garden she made there became a source of inspiration for her work.

Conversely one can admire, appreciate and enjoy a trip to Petworth Park without a full historical grasp of the lives and loves of the various Lords Egremont and Leconfield.

## House and garden

Of even greater importance than the relationship of garden to maker must be that of context. No garden appears by accident. Most gardens were created as adjuncts to a building, such as a house, a priory or a country seat. Often these buildings dictate the style of the garden. However, the notion of a 'period garden' is always contentious, no garden can be preserved in aspic. Gardens are living things, always changing and subject to change: proving particularly vulnerable to the vicissitudes of natural phenomena such as drought, disease and unusual storms.

When visiting a garden it adds greatly to one's understanding and appreciation if it is considered in relation to its built environment, as this is often its *RAISON D'ÊTRE*. This can be problematic as some gardens have, over time, become annexed from their original building. This has happened at Highdown which has become detached from the home of its creator; Kipling Gardens has also been annexed from its neighbouring house, although here the original garden walls still dictate its configuration. Some gardens, such as Great Dixter, are impossible to imagine without their accompanying buildings, so integral are they to the site. By contrast Merriments Garden makes no reference to anything but itself whilst Marchants Hardy Plants makes a direct and very effective reference not to a building but to the downland landscape beyond. Due to their favoured locations many Sussex gardens look outward to the surrounding countryside and 'borrow' views from beyond their boundaries (both Alfriston Clergy House and Monk's House benefit greatly not just from the Downs but also from neighbouring churches). Others, such as Denmans Garden, are far more contained and inward looking. Where a chosen garden is attached to a building it is not always possible to visit both, however, if access is available I have indicated this in the text. Many certainly are worth seeing if time allows and will add another dimension to your garden visit.

## Swings and arrows

In looking at these gardens several themes recurred across the county and it is interesting to compare how events have impacted on various gardens in different ways. Sussex has always been an essentially rural county. Even today there are few really large urban centres, our cities tend to be of small size and the landscape has not been scarred by industrial processes such as mining or steel production. On the contrary in several instances the spoils of agricultural or industrial disruption have been utilised and turned into lovely gardens. An example is the former chalk pits and quarries that presented the makers of the gardens at Highdown, Standen and the Italian Gardens at Eastbourne with opportunities to create new exciting garden spaces. Similarly areas of many large Sussex gardens were ploughed up and cultivated as vegetable plots during the First and Second World Wars as part of the very successful, and vital, Dig For Victory campaign. Once peace had returned many gardeners saw these newly flattened areas as opportunities to develop new ideas and features in their now safe corner of England.

Over the centuries Sussex has been favoured with a number of wealthy inhabitants whose passions were plants rather than more questionable pursuits of pleasure. Consequently many of the county's gardens benefited from their owner's generous sponsorship of the expeditions of great plant hunters such as Frank Kingdon-Ward, Ernest Henry Wilson, Reginald Farrer and George Forrest. Certainly Borde Hill and Highdown would be lesser places today without their contributions, whilst the founding of a charitable trust by Edward James has allowed both the house and gardens at West Dean to survive and flourish.

However, Nature has not always shown the same benevolence towards Sussex and has inflicted two particularly cruel assaults on the county's population of trees. Dutch elm disease spread to Britain in the mid-1960s and has devastated the sheltering elms that once graced so many gardens and enhanced so many country lanes. By the 1990s it was estimated that over 25 million trees had been lost across the country. Miraculously there are survival pockets of mature English elms, notably in the Brighton and Hove area. Elsewhere this has naturally led to the replacement planting of other species and as time progresses one can only hope that a greater variety of mature trees will offer some recompense for the sad losses. The other terrible blow, quite literally, to befall the trees of Sussex was the Great Storm of 1987. The worst storm to lash south-east England since 1703 hit the coast during the early hours of 16th October and uprooted 15 million trees. Again and again as you read accounts of the gardens in this book I am afraid that the tree-felling spectre of the storm will appear with depressing regularity.

## Some practical advice on visiting gardens

I have avoided citing opening times as it is impossible to be accurate from year to year. Although open broadly for the same period each year many garden opening times are tied to such movable feasts as Easter and vagaries such as 'dusk'. Therefore do always check with the garden before embarking on a visit (telephone numbers and website details are provided as available). Likewise detailed information on entrance fees, access for the disabled, parking, toilet facilities, tea rooms and whether or not dogs are welcome can all be obtained from the garden direct. National grid references have been supplied for all the gardens and an indication of the availability of public transport. Again, the people who run the individual gardens really are the experts here and are always happy to advise on the best methods for travelling to their venue. Many gardens in this book are in the country and public transport in rural areas can be variable and somewhat unpredictable so again do check with the provider.

One of the criteria used in choosing the gardens for this book is the maximum provision of access for visitors over a long season. In the Other Gardens to Visit section I list many other gardens again that are frequently open to the public and are certainly worth visiting. However, of necessity this has meant omitting some wonderful gardens, usually privately owned, that are only accessible for limited periods. Many of these are open under the auspices of the National Gardens Scheme (NGS). This admirable nationwide organisation oversees the opening of private as well as public gardens on selected dates from February to October. All proceeds go to predominantly nursing and gardening charities. They publish annually a guide to gardens open under the scheme throughout the country as well as a booklet that just deals with Sussex NGS gardens. The NGS embraces all kinds of gardens, from the smallest urban plot to the grandest country estate; the uniting element is the passion, dedication and enthusiasm of their owners which will provide visitors with endless inspiration (and often provoke not a little envy!) It is a rare privilege to be invited into such private spaces and one that always repays the effort. Many of the gardens I have selected for this guide are also participants of the scheme so should the visitor wish to contribute to the work of the NGS they should select their dates accordingly.

So, armed with this guide I wish you many long and happy months of garden outings. Certainly my visits to these places have confirmed my long-held view that the making of gardens is one of the better things that men and women do! It is indeed as Francis Bacon puts it, 'the purest of human pleasures'.

# BATEMAN'S

## BURWASH

The author Rudyard Kipling (*1865-1936*) fled with his family to live at Bateman's in 1902 when the intrusions into their private lives that they suffered at his former home at Rottingdean on the Sussex coast became too much (*see p.43*). At the time, he wrote of the 17th-century house, 'We have loved it ever since our first sight of it', a sentiment most visitors will feel some sympathy with today. This beautiful solid and sheltering mellow house was constructed in 1634 using local sandstone, quarried just across the lane, while the tiles covering the ample roof are made from Wealden clay. Kipling lived here until his death and the house, garden and surrounding Dudwell valley became a rich source for his work. In particular his collected children's stories *Puck of Pook's Hill*, 1906, and *Rewards and Fairies*, 1910, draw heavily on the immediate area surrounding Bateman's.

When the house was purchased in 1902 only 13 hectares accompanied it. By 1928 Kipling had pursued such an active policy of land acquisition that he was the proud owner of 121 hectares, creating an effective *cordon sanitaire* between him and the world outside. Within the privacy afforded by the high stone walls, the gardens were extensively developed and improved, under the close supervision of Kipling.

Overall this is a garden of restraint, exuding a sense of calm and timelessness. One feels a gentle autumn day would see it at its best; long shadows, leaves just on the turn, a slight chill in the air, the whiff of a distant bonfire, all the things that conjure up an English country garden of the southern counties.

The garden is now entered through the Orchard. This was the former kitchen garden and a substantial area is still in cultivation, growing a variety of vegetables and flowers for cutting. Innovative ways of growing the winter squash 'Turk's Turban' were evident on my visit. These rampant trailers were being trained up and over an elevated frame. As the plants run along the horizontal supports the fruits hang down, their full exoticism displayed to its best advantage. Along the right side of the Orchard runs a very long herb border, full of both medicinal and culinary varieties, all well identified. The lawns are dotted with old fruit trees and are intersected by a rose-covered pergola. An informal hedge of rugosa roses screens some of the vegetables. Evidence of Kipling's not inconsiderable garden-design skills can be seen in the unusual Pear Alley or Arch. This aligns with the iron gates that lead to the enclosed walled garden beyond and consists of a long alley formed from the generous spread of iron arches. These support 22 espaliered pears including the varieties 'Conference', 'Superfine' and 'Winter Nelis', underplanted with groundcover. A wide brick path terminates in a very attractive seat with brickwork sides and arched back. Before proceeding through the iron gates (into which the initials 'RK' have been decoratively worked), note the row of simple small-flowered varieties of fuchsias that grow along the base of the walls on either side of the gateway – an excellent example of the restrained but effective planting that is such a hallmark of this garden.

Through the gateway lies the Mulberry Garden. Although Kipling planted a mulberry here in 1905, the tree we see today is obviously a much newer replacement although it is accompanied by much older pears and apples. Designed by Kipling, and formerly a wagon yard, this enclosed area now contains all the classic ingredients of a traditional walled garden; high brick walls, low box hedging and mixed herbaceous planting, much of it fragrant. The beds were redesigned for the National Trust by Graham Stuart Thomas. Old and worn mill stones have been set into the main path and a high yew arch marks the exit.

The house lies ahead and is well worth a visit, the interior being quite as inviting as its façade, as its former inhabitant noted 'a real House in which to settle down for keeps.' Tucked away just behind the house are two former oast-houses and dovecote (now home to the shop). As at Great Dixter (*see p. 35*) these buildings, along with the roofs and chimneys of Bateman's, lend a wonderfully romantic backdrop to the garden. A plain and simple formal lawn, with its sentinel Irish yews and hedges, stretches out before the front of the house to the entrance gate and to the lane beyond.

Leaving the house by the southern exit brings one into the most impressive and unique part of the garden at Bateman's. From a generous stone terrace a large expanse of lawn lies ahead with two rows of parallel pleached limes that run away from the house. These were planted in 1898, so predate Kipling's time here. The higher area is known as the Quarter Deck and is separated from the lower part by a low drystone retaining wall. This change in level acts as something of a flood defence against the sometimes encroaching River Dudwell.

Beyond the western row of limes is the Pond and Rose Garden designed by Kipling as a place for the children to boat and swim. The development of the area was funded by the proceeds of his 1907 Nobel Prize money (the then princely sum of £7,700). The rectangular pool is full of water-lilies, mimulus, water mint, irises and bull rushes and, now emptied of children, is very tranquil. A formally arranged Rose Garden is at the farthest end of the pond and behind a sundial is set into a semi-circular niche in the bordering yew hedge, with the Kiplingesque legend 'it is later than you think'. Directly opposite across the pond another niche echoes this but has a semi-circular wooden seat set within it.

Hidden within the stretch of hedge which forms the southern boundary is access to the Wild Garden. This is romantic and shaded providing a contrasting change of mood from the bright and open geometric order around the house. Formally the site of old grass tennis courts, meandering paths have been mowed through trees and sweet-smelling and flowering shrubs. Early in the year spring bulbs and wild flowers precede the blooms of rhododendrons and azaleas. Hidden in one corner is a small collection of graves of former Kipling family pets. The River Dudwell runs through the Wild Garden and the largest gunnera I have ever seen growing in this country thrives in its shallow waters. A bridge leads to a path that takes the visitor to the working watermill. In Kipling's time it was used to power electricity, now flour is ground here from local corn.

Kipling and his family left The Elms at Rottingdean partly because it was so full of memories of his young daughter Josephine who died of pneumonia aged six. Sadly their time at Bateman's was not to be unmarked by tragedy as in 1915 their son John was reported missing at the Battle of Loos. Both Kipling and his wife Carrie were profoundly changed by these tragic losses and perhaps something of this sadness still pervades this lovely corner of the Sussex Weald.

**Getting there**                                   National grid ref. TQ671238
- Burwash, Etchingham, East Sussex, TN19 7DS.
- National Trust, tel 01435 882302, website: www.nationaltrust.org.uk
- Limited bus service to Burwash from Heathfield and Etchingham.
- Two miles (three kilometres) from Etchingham Station.
- **Other gardens nearby:** Great Dixter (see page 35), Merriments (see page 53), Pashley Manor Gardens.

# BORDE HILL

## HAYWARDS HEATH

T he gardens, park, woodland and lakes of Borde Hill occupy 80 hectares of prime Sussex countryside overlooking the High Weald and provide the garden visitor with interest whatever the time of year. The varied façade of Borde Hill House looks southwards over rolling lawns, beyond the ha-ha to the South Park while the North Park, with its ambling woodland walks, lies behind. The woodland and lakes offer the visitor a wide range of activities but the extensive gardens alone certainly repay a visit and are something of a treasure trove for any self-respecting tree spotter.

Borde Hill House is a Tudor mansion dating back to 1580 although it was substantially altered in the 19th century. Colonel Stephenson Robert Clarke purchased the estate in 1893 and was responsible for developing much of what we see in the garden today. An avid naturalist and keen patron of many of the great plant hunters of the period, Clarke fully utilised the newly introduced plant varieties from the intrepid collectors' expeditions to such diverse habitats as China, Burma, the Himalayas, Tasmania and the Andes. All the great names contributed to the stock at Borde Hill including Ernest Henry Wilson, Reginald Farrer, George Forrest, Frank Kingdom-Ward and Dr. Joseph Rock, while Harold Comber, son of James Comber the head gardener at nearby Nymans (*see p. 59*), introduced Andean and Tasmanian plants in the 1920s. Clarke's descendants still own and run Borde Hill and subsequent generations have continued to restore, develop and improve the grounds. The garden became a charity in 1965 overseen by representatives of the Royal Horticultural Society, the Forestry Commission and the Royal Botanic Gardens, so its exotic treasures are certainly in safe hands.

The gardens at Borde Hill are many and varied, each with its own particular emphasis and atmosphere. Yet the scale of the grounds and landscape balance this diversity and each area adds to rather than detracts from the whole. This is deep rhodo country and spring brings wonderful displays of rhododendrons, azaleas, camellias and magnolias, all of which look stunning in this natural setting. In sharp contrast is the Jay Robin's Rose Garden. This is an example of a traditional English rose garden at its best yet was only designed (by Robin Williams) and planted in 1996. It has been created in the style of the original rose garden that featured in a 1902 *Country Life* article. A central circular fountain provides the focal point while low box and lavender hedging, brick paths and tall yew topiary delineate the layout. Over 100 varieties of David Austin English roses fill the beds in a profusion of colour and scent. Alongside the Rose Garden runs a long herbaceous border with a Shady Garden beyond, also designed by Robin Williams. Here, sheltered by the old fern house, is a marble statue known variously as the Veiled Lady or the Bride, *c.*1800. The work of Milanese sculptor Antonio Tantardini, it used to stand, appropriately, in the Italian Garden. Something of a period piece, her rather baroque swooning excesses are probably not much suited to many modern tastes. In contrast the serried rows of light blue obelisks that support white climbers strike a more contemporary note. A smaller area has been developed as a White Garden, providing a cool foil to the multi-hued roses.

More blue trelliswork, this time in the shape of a supporting arch, leads into the delightful Mediterranean Garden. This is a really successful space, its boundaries formed by the old walls of a Victorian greenhouse. Paving stones are laid in gravel from which architectural plants such as phormiums, artichokes and a large Japanese plum (*Eriobotrya japonica)* grow. A lovely collection of Grecian pots contain plants such as agave, sage, fennel and agapanthus. Large specimens of Chisan palm (*Trachycarpus fortunei*) and Italian cypress (*Cupressus sempervirens*) complete the southern theme.

Heritage Lottery money has generously funded the restoration of a number of the Victorian greenhouses that, along with the potting sheds, were once at the working heart of this garden. Before World War II, Borde Hill employed 27 full-time gardeners, now there are six. Exotic species, many originating from Africa, inhabit the largest of the greenhouses including a collection of aloes, a splendid *Strelitzia* and many pots of *Streptocarpus* in an impressive array of gradations of blue. A towering *Cyperus papyrus* stands in a pot by the door displaying its beautiful fronds. From late summer to autumn the collection of nerines, originally developed by Mrs Stephenson Clarke in the post-war period, can be found in flower while peaches grow happily in the smaller greenhouse. Outside in this area several apple trees grow in large pots. Their obvious health, vigour and prolific fruiting should encourage anyone with only a small garden or terrace to attempt to produce their own crop in such a way.

The Long Walk follows the southern boundary created by the ha-ha and is a delight to stroll along in any season with its mixed and varied planting. Some of the most intriguing enclosed gardens at Borde Hill are accessed from here, lying just to the north of the Long Walk. What is now the Italian Garden was once home to the family's tennis court. The rectangular central pool was introduced in the early 1980s and the Italian theme has continued to be developed. Wide stone and brick paths surround the water-lily-filled pool and a small basin fountain provides the gentle sound of trickling water. This is augmented by the rill that descends from a semi-circular pool down several steps and feeds into the main pond. This is one of the best designed modern rills I have seen and has been extremely well executed. Low box hedging and tall cypresses add to the Italian atmosphere bringing something of the Campania to the Sussex Weald.

After the open geometric order of the Italian Garden the gothic delights of the Round Dell offer a sharp change of mood. A meandering set of stone steps (uneven in places so suited only to the sure-footed) takes a circuitous route around a central pool which in summer is almost obscured by giant rhubarb (*Gunnera manicata*). This densely planted area creates a micro-climate hospitable to many sub-tropical herbaceous perennials and exotic trees such as palms and bananas. Rustling bamboos add to the sensory delights. A fine bronze statue of a young female figure lifting her arms up in joy to the sun and sky nestles in among the cannas, astilbes and miscanthus.

At the end of the Long Walk are the Old Potting Sheds. What was once an extensive collection of interconnected working brick sheds is now home to many tender species of plants common to the southern hemisphere. In what is an unusual variation on the walled garden, only the part-ruined walls of the old potting sheds remain, their roofs removed and the gardeners' working paraphernalia replaced with raised beds, integral seats and stone sinks planted with alpines. While a table made from an old millstone adds a domestic note in one of the 'rooms'.

Heading northwards from the sheds lies the Long Dell, a former stone quarry planted with trees and shrubs from the Sino-Himalayan region. Beyond here is the area that will be of particular interest to aficionados of rhododendrons, as many unusual and rare specimens thrive at Borde Hill. The official guide book is unusually fulsome in its listing of the various species. To the north west of the house is the Garden of Allah. Dating from 1925 its name was coined by Colonel Sir Ralph Stephenson Clarke who considered the area so tranquil that one might have 'met Allah around the next bush'! More unusual rhododendrons flourish here, many introduced by Kingdom-Ward (two of which flower in summer). There are also mature survivors of seeds originally sent by Forrest and Rock from South-West Yunnan and the borders of Burma and Tibet. Several of Borde Hill's champion trees also occupy this peaceful spot and an elevated gazebo, known as Becky's Bower, provides a sheltered seat from which to enjoy the peace. Signposted woodland walks into the parkland can be started from here. To the east of the house are the Azalea and Camellia Rings. May is the time to enjoy the impressive collection of azaleas, predominantly of the Knapp Hill strain, although there are many fine and interesting shrubs and trees in this area so there is always something to enjoy.

Many of the plants and particularly the trees at Borde Hill are of considerable horticultural merit, several are the original or oldest living specimens in the country. This longevity can be attributed to their having been planted in the most appropriate and favourable habitat, rather than having been grouped with other varieties simply for visual effect. Borde Hill has a range of soil conditions, from heavy clay to the more auspicious light loam. The gardens also boast an impressive collection of over 100 champion trees; that is, measured specimens that are either the tallest or the widest of girth in Britain today. A comprehensive list of the trees and their measurements can be found on the website and a very helpful free leaflet identifies and describes the Plant Hunter's Woodland Tree Trail in Stephanie's Glade and Warren Wood.

All in all a very full, informative and enjoyable day can be spent at Borde Hill Gardens.

**Getting there**                                        National grid ref. TQ324264
- Balcombe Road, Haywards Heath, West Sussex, RH16 1XP.
- Tel 01444 450326, website: www.bordehill.co.uk
- Nearest station Haywards Heath.
- **Other gardens nearby:** High Beeches Gardens, Nymans Garden (see page 59), Sheffied Park Garden, Wakehurst Place.

# CHARLESTON & MONK'S HOUSE

## FIRLE & RODMELL

The cultural, artistic and literary life of Sussex during the first half of the 20th century is inescapably linked with that coterie of artists and writers now collectively known as the 'Bloomsbury Group'. Not only did they paint, write and decorate their houses in innovative and daring ways but they also made gardens. Two of the most notable examples, Charleston Farmhouse and Monk's House, are open to the public and both are well worth a visit both as adjuncts to two cultural domestic icons and as lovely gardens in their own right.

### Charleston Farmhouse

Charleston Farmhouse was the country home of the painters Vanessa Bell (*1879-1961*) and Duncan Grant (*1885-1978*) from 1916 until the latter's death in 1978. First rented as a rural retreat from the twin dangers of London bombs and conscription, the house was retained as a holiday home during the inter-war years, finally moving there permanently in 1939. Throughout the years the house and garden provided a welcoming setting for a houseguest list that reads like a Who's Who of English intellectual and artistic life in the first half of the 20th century. Leonard and Virginia Woolf (Bell's sister), Lytton Strachey, John Maynard Keynes, T.S. Elliot, Benjamin Britten – these are just a few of the illustrious names who made the journey up the country lane to the pretty farmhouse at the foot of the Downs.

The garden was an overgrown jungle of potatoes and old apple trees in 1916 but Vanessa Bell oversaw its transformation into a delightful sheltered oasis planted with an artist's eye for colour and form. The garden is entered through an unassuming pair of gates which are flanked by posts topped with copies of a pair of urns designed and made by Vanessa's younger son Quentin. Directly opposite the front of the house is the old farm pond, now lush with water lilies and marginal planting. The far side of the pond is home to two sculptures, a levitating figure and a female figure, also by Quentin. A magnificent *Magnolia grandiflora* scrambles over the mellow façade of the house, along with roses.

A gate in the wall to the right of the house leads into the lovely large flint-walled garden. Several casts of classical heads decorate the tops of the garden walls, copies of those originally collected and placed there by Duncan. Here a profusion of plants compete for attention, creating a riot of colour from spring until late autumn. Several narrow paths intersect the garden and meet the overgrown box hedge at the far side, now trimmed into a softly undulating mass of curves. Set within this hedge is a cast of the Venus de Milo placed to terminate a long vista when viewed from the house.

Behind the hedge lies one of the most unique features of the garden, a terrace originally designed by the art critic and painter Roger Fry and known as the Piazza. The concrete terrace floor is decorated with mosaics made from broken brick and ceramics, created by Duncan and Vanessa along with her children, Quentin and Angelica, and their friend Janie Bussey in 1946. This corner suntrap is cooled by the trickling fountain which feeds a small semi-circular pool decorated with tiles by Quentin. Also behind the box hedge is a small decorative potager, filled with artichokes, strawberries, sweet peas and sun-flowers. The profusion of the planting is relieved by an area of lawn which contains a pretty sunken pool edged with copies of tiles originally designed by Vanessa.

The house is open to the public and informative guided tours provide the visitor with a glimpse of the highly creative, if somewhat unorthodox, domestic arrangements enjoyed by its erstwhile inhabitants. However, the garden alone can be visited, along with the shop (where specially packaged packets of Charleston-style flowers such as zinnias and holly-hocks can be bought), gallery and tearoom. In fine weather tea can be taken in the delightful tiny walled garden known as the Folly, which was originally accessed from Duncan's studio.

## Monk's House

From 1919 Monk's House was the Sussex retreat of the writers Leonard (*1880-1969*) and Virginia Woolf (*1882-1941*). Sadly it was from here that Virginia started on her final journey in March 1941 which ended in the nearby waters of the River Ouse. Leonard lived on in the house until his death in 1969. Just like the garden at Charleston Farmhouse, in its heyday the Monk's House garden frequently provided a congenial backdrop to gatherings of many of the distinguished writers and artists of the Bloomsbury Group. Their visitors included the writer and creator of Sissinghurst, Vita Sackville-West, a close friend of Virginia.

In her diaries Virginia describes Monk's House as 'an unpretending house, long and low' and indeed for such a modest 18th-century Sussex cottage, the very large garden seems somewhat disproportionate. This is explained by the purchase in 1928 of the adjoining Pond Croft Field, thus doubling the size of the original plot. The garden was very much the preserve of Leonard and to locals he was a familiar figure, often to be seen working in the large vegetable patch. The area that was once the kitchen garden is now let to local allotment holders and so continues to be expertly tended. Leonard loved flowers and indulged a passion for growing exotics in a palette of hot colours. He employed a full-time gardener, plus occasional help, and oversaw the cultivation of the flowers, vegetables, greenhouses, beehives and orchard.

The well-utilised glasshouse runs virtually the whole length of the long cottage at the rear. Inside can be seen a copy of Donatello's *David* that used to grace the garden. From the house rises an elaborate, if somewhat uneven, series of brick terraces. These are punctured with well-stocked beds, over-brimming pots and old fruit trees. The remains of the walls of old agricultural buildings form intimate spaces containing seating areas and a small sunken lily pond. From here stroll through the lush archway into a large expanse of grass with a dewpond and sculpture of *Goliath* by C.H.N. Mommen, *c.* 1935. This is the site of the Woolfs' much-used bowling green.

Behind the formal terrace is an old orchard, which is thickly carpeted with daffodils in spring. The exceedingly pretty 12th-century church of St Peter's lies in view just beyond the garden's low flint walls. Beehives complete the bucolic scene. The building at the far end of the orchard is Virginia's writing room, known as the lodge, and is strategically placed with views to the water meadows and Downs. Open to the public, extracts from her diaries, along with photographs, are on display here.

Within the garden a low wall provides the modest support for lead-cast busts of the famous former inhabitants of Monk's House. The one of Virginia is by Stephen Tomlin, 1931 (the original is at Charleston), and that of Leonard by Charlotte Hewer, 1968. Originally two great elm trees, known as Leonard and Virginia, grew in the hedge beyond the dewpond. It was here that Virginia's ashes were scattered. However, both trees grow no longer: one came down in a storm in 1943 and the second sadly succumbed to Dutch elm disease in 1985.

The house is open to the public and has much the same spirit and style that is evident at Charleston Farmhouse. Indeed the two properties and their accompanying gardens compliment one another well and, when opening times coincide, make for a stimulating afternoon out.

---

**Getting to Charleston**                    National grid ref. TQ490069

- Near Firle, East Sussex, BN8 6LL.
- The Charleston Trust, tel 01323 811265, website: www.charleston.org.uk
- East of Lewes on the A27. Two mile (three kilometre) walk from Berwick Station.
- Limited bus service from Lewes and the Cuckmere Community Bus.

**Getting to Monk's House**                    National grid ref. TQ417063

- Rodmell, East Sussex, BN7 3HF.
- The National Trust, tel 01273 474760, website: www.nationaltrust.org.uk
- **Other gardens nearby:** Alfriston Clergy House (*see page 25*), Marchants Hardy Plants (*see page 49*), Michelham Priory (*see page 56*), Wellingham Herb Garden, Southover Grange.

# CLERGY HOUSE

## ALFRISTON

The Cuckmere Valley is thought by many to be the most attractive river valley in the county and Alfriston Clergy House must surely occupy one of the most picturesque positions alongside the banks of the Cuckmere River. The house and garden enjoy stunning vistas across the river, to the South Downs and of the imposing spire of nearby St Andrew's Church, long known as 'the cathedral of the Downs'.

This timber-framed Wealden hall house has a fascinating history. The Clergy House may date from as early as 1350, certainly from the 15th century it was in the possession of Michelham Priory (*see p.56*), only a few kilometres away. Time took its toll on the building and by the late 19th century the Church authorities reported it as near derelict. Demolition seemed a likely option. The local vicar, the Reverend F. W. Benyon, was outraged at the prospect of losing such a fine example of Sussex vernacular building and set up an appeal to save it.

Both the Sussex Archaeological Society and the Society for the Protection of Ancient Buildings supported Benyon's efforts to save the Clergy House. Funds were raised and work began. In 1896 the building was sold to the newly formed National Trust for just £10. Thus Alfriston Clergy House became the first historic building to be acquired and restored by the Trust.

The building's rich architectural palette of thatch, brick, flint, hung clay tiles and exposed timber framing can be glimpsed enticingly over tall hedges as visitors arrive on the pretty village green, known locally as the Tye. The garden, which surrounds the house on all sides, was laid out in the 1920s by Sir Robert Witt. Sir Robert, who founded the Witt Photographic Library, was the first of the Trust's many tenants. Since 1977 the house and garden have been open to the public.

Although the garden extends over a considerable area it is divided into a series of intimate spaces, all essentially planted in the cottage-garden style. The size of these spaces seems particularly appropriate and fitting to the scale of the house. It is these smaller areas that will provide visitors to the Clergy House garden with ample inspiration for their own domestic plots. The garden's layout deals extremely successfully with changes of level, incorporating varied configurations of tiles, bricks and checkerboard flints in a series of steps, retaining walls and edges. These are deployed with particular success in the herb garden. Also note the use of large terracotta pots throughout the garden. Here an excellent balance of scale between pot and garden space exists, not always an easy feat to achieve.

The beds which flank the narrow entrance to the property overflow in herbaceous profusion in the summer months. The garden then descends on the left into an area of lawn and orchard. Fortunately the garden's impressive Judas tree (*Cercis siliquastrum*) just survived the ravages of the 1987 hurricane and blooms profusely in early June. Old varieties of apple, quince, medlar and mulberry still fruit here every year. Spring sees the emergence of bulbs, including the snake's head fritillaria, while in early summer serpentine paths are mown through the ox-eye daisies.

The river forms the southern boundary of the garden and provides a lovely walk for the visitor, with the water on one side and a raised herbaceous border on the other. This is richly planted with old cottage garden favourites including columbines, hardy geraniums, hyssop, poppies, pinks, rock roses, achilleas and all are framed by a wondrous array of roses.

Rising up a short flight of steps is the herb garden where the plants thrive in the sheltered southern aspect. From here the most distinctive area of the garden is reached, this contrasting formal area to the west of the house is completely enclosed by tall clipped yew hedging. At the centre of the cruciform narrow brick paths is a sundial surrounded by four very large clipped box trees, underplanted with old-fashioned pinks. These impressive trees are so old that they are multi-stemmed and will come as something of a surprise to anyone who only associates box with low formal hedging!

Beyond the tall yew hedges lies an attractive potager with raised beds constructed from railway sleepers. Alongside the usual potatoes and rhubarb and the less usual artichokes, grow an array of flowers for cutting and a nursery bed of box and beech plants. Currants are grown in large pots and have been placed to terminate the axes of the paths between the vegetable beds.

This is a garden that fits well both with the very individual Clergy House and within its setting. It is divided into a series of spaces that provide differing moods and aspects yet each seems to flow effortlessly into the next. This cleverly belies the tightly designed structure beneath and all is softened by the colourful generosity of the billowing planting. The whole experience is considerably enhanced by the lovely riverside setting and visitors should allow some time to visit the nearby St Andrew's Church and enjoy a stroll down the pretty village high street.

**Getting there**                                      National grid ref. TQ521029
- The Tye, Alfriston, Polegate, East Sussex, BN26 5TL.
- National Trust, tel 01323 871961, website: www.nationaltrust.org.uk
- Bus from Eastbourne, Seaford and Lewes. Cuckmere Community Bus at weekends.
- Two and a half miles (four kilometres) from Berwick Station.
- **Other gardens nearby:** Herstmonceux Castle, Marchants Hardy Plants (see page 49), Michelham Priory (see page 56), Charleston Farmhouse (see page 21).

# DENMANS GARDEN

## FONTWELL

Denmans perhaps has one of the least promising approaches of any garden featured in this book. After turning off the main road the visitor must take a short tour through a collection of old farm buildings, now converted to commercial use, before arriving at the entrance to the garden. Once through the gate, however, all is transformed and a green and lush plantsman's haven is revealed accompanied by a very enticing plant centre. John Brookes, the internationally renowned garden designer, lecturer and writer, has been based at Denmans Garden since 1980. Here he has created an innovative, stimulating and very beautiful series of spaces that provide endless inspiration for the visitor. The 1.6-hectare site originally formed part of the home farm of the estate of Lord Denman in the 19th century. Its origins as the garden we see today date back to 1946 when Joyce Robinson and her husband purchased the area, retaining the two cottages, clock house and garden. Brookes took over the running of the garden in 1981. However, the redoubtable Mrs Robinson continued to live at Denmans and could often be seen inspecting the garden from her wheelchair until her death in 1996.

The garden is approached via a large Dutch greenhouse, originally designed to raise strawberries, tomatoes and flowers for sale. It is now host to a variety of frost-tender species, among them a large agave and several exotic-looking yuccas. The semi-tropical feel of the greenhouse sits particularly well with the garden beyond. Denmans is on the well-drained, gravelly soil so typical of its downland location and sun-loving Mediterranean plants thrive here.

The Walled Garden is an enclosed oasis of colour, fragrance and form and much of the key elements of Brookes's planting style can be seen here: a heady mix of generously planted perennials and herbs arranged in a deceptively casual way but anchored by an underlying formal plan. Giant box balls, glorious tree peonies (whenever I see these lovely plants I wonder why they aren't grown more often), stately verbascums, impressive cardoons, all grow beautifully here and the result is a layering of one shape, colour and form of foliage on top of another, creating a great sense of depth and lushness. The sheltering flint walls are adorned with old-fashioned roses and these tall walls help trap the delightful scents that waft around the visitor. The use of gravel features throughout the garden, both as paths and as a planting medium and certainly many of the plants grown in the Walled Garden seem particularly suited to this dry, stony groundcover. Note Brookes's use and interplay of scale when arranging plants; tall species abound here and not just at the back of the borders.

Perhaps the most distinctive feature of Denmans is the Dry Stream Bed. Originally created by Mrs Robinson in 1977 it has been extended over the years. A lovely sinuous 'stream' of dry gravel intersects the open aspect of lawn and is planted with appropriate species. The conditions here are perfect for self-seeders which, with deceptively careful editing, help create the illusion of totally natural planting. In the 1980s a pond was made which terminates the 'stream' and now provides a home to a family of moorhens.

The South Garden has a more informal feel, paths are mown through the long grass, planted with bulbs and wild flowers. As Denmans is open all year the whole garden is planted in such a way as to provide the maximum seasonal interest. The Top Lawn has a formal circular pond, surrounded by tender species. A Dawn Redwood (*Metasequoia*) makes an impressive statement on the lawn while throughout the garden tall palms, both green and bronze, add vertical accents to the wide beds.

Two standard bay trees with corkscrew trunks stand guard outside the conservatory which houses chattering budgerigars as well as succulents!

From here the clock house, a former stable block, can be seen across the lawn. This is the home and studio of John Brookes and also houses his landscape school. One of the delights encountered by visitors to Denmans is the unexpected discovery of various sculptures strategically placed around the garden. Spot the odd relaxed seated figure or a gaggle of geese; these are the work of sculptor Marion Smith. Along with these static fowl many of their live cousins, in the form of rare breed poultry, enliven the garden.

**Getting there**                                              National grid ref. SU945070
❯ Denmans Lane, Fontwell, West Sussex, BN18 0SU.
❯ John Brookes, tel 01243 542808, website: www.denmans-garden.co.uk
❯ East of Chichester on the A27, three miles (five kilometres) from Barnham Station.
❯ **Other gardens nearby:** Arundel Castle, Uppark, Weald & Downland Open Air Museum, West Dean (see page 82).

# EASTBOURNE SEAFRONT

## EASTBOURNE

Perhaps not immediately thought of by most as 'a garden to visit' in the traditional sense, yet the many and varied green spaces that run the length of Eastbourne seafront can provide as much enjoyment and interest as more conventional gardens, and with the added bonus of a little bracing exercise! A leisurely stroll from east of the pier along to the most westerly point of the promenade reveals a surprising range of planting often immaculately executed and expertly tended. Many of the gardens are separate entities and have been treated very much as themed areas in their own right, while the more expansive beds that run alongside the road and the promenade often feature schemes in which the same key plants have been repeated, thus giving a coherence to the whole. The cultivated areas that run from east and west of the pier are rather different in character; generally the eastwards side is more ornate and colourful while the westward end is more architectural and, dare one say, artistic in feel.

Starting in the east opposite the Treasure Island attraction is the Tank Enclosure Garden. This relatively small area will be of particular interest to all those gardeners who have suffered from drought conditions in the recent dry and hot summers. Beneath the lawns and flower beds lies the town's storm water drainage system, fortunately making the site unsuitable for development but perfect for a garden. In previous years traditional bedding schemes were planted here annually. However, more recently a greater environmentally sustainable regime has been adopted which does not rely on artificial watering. Mixed planting through gravel of cabbage palms (*Cordyline*), variegated agaves, red hot pokers (*kniphofia*), cardoons, yuccas, perovskia and sedums all lend a tropical feel. This area is enclosed and cannot be entered but it is only surrounded by a low wall so can easily be viewed from all sides.

Continue along the seafront but before reaching the pier look for the Metropole Triangle Garden which lies across the road set back within a three-sided square. In the true spirit of holiday fun this garden fully acknowledges its seaside location and seems to hark back to a former, more innocent, age. Here a floral boat and lighthouse float amid a sea of lawn and colourful bedding schemes, the latter changed each spring and summer. The lighthouse is a replica of its neighbouring counterpart at Beachy Head; its 'walls' are constructed of houseleeks and it sits amid a semi-circular 'reef' of rocks and old wooden breakers, flowers and even an old lobster pot.

From the pier it is easy to locate the impressive Carpet Gardens just to the west. Once the stalwart of public parks throughout the country, it is now a rare sight to see well executed carpet-bedding schemes. It was the Victorians, with their armies of highly skilled gardeners, who developed the technique of carpet bedding. Elaborate patterns, often geometric and reminiscent of rugs, are created using huge numbers of low growing foliage and flowering plants arranged in close proximity. It is painstaking and intricate work that requires continued high main-tenance. At Eastbourne the theme changes from year to year but is always impressive. Even if such schemes are not to your taste, their relative rarity these days lends them a novelty interest and value.

At this point the promenade splits into higher and lower levels. On the lower ground either side of the bandstand are mixed shrub beds and rockeries where a huge range of plants aim to provide year-round inter-est. Moroccan broom (*Cytisus battandieri*), the daisy bush (*Olearia macrodonta*), flowering currant (*Ribes speciosum*) can all be found here punctuated with yet more large cabbage palms. These will provide plen-tiful inspiration for anyone gardening in coastal conditions as the beds get year-round salt-laden drying winds and harsh exposure to sun, yet still seem to flower and thrive.

Eastbourne (along with Worthing) often boasts that it is the sunniest place in the country and the tropical mood of the Wish Tower Borders serves only to reinforce this view. They are reached by taking the gentle slope up onto an expanse of lawn which is set with large areas of shrubs and flowers, while below the long border runs along the lower edge and divides the lawns from the pavement and road. Stately architectural yuccas, agaves, Canary (*Phoenix canariensis*) and cabbage palms all thrive here. Salvias and cannas contribute welcome splashes of intense colour.

Continue walking westwards on the higher level. This is a wide pathway sheltered to the right by high rocky walls which overspill with lush shrubs and trees. The coastal side is protected by a lovely loose screen of tamarisk (*Tamarix*) and laurel (*Prunus laurocerasus*) with views to the sea beyond, while ahead are the nearby Downs and the familiar Sussex cliffs. This delightful path has nothing of the tightly tended municipal seaside about it. Rather, with its soft gravel surface, the gentle lapping sound of the sea and the rustling of the tamarisk, it feels much more like a chic and sophisticated Mediterranean resort than the windswept south coast of England. This area makes for a particularly enticing stroll in the evening when the regularly spaced lamp posts give off a magical gentle glow. Frequent pathways, with quaint names such as Fir Tree Cross, intersect the cliffs going down to the lower promenade and beach and also up to the lawns and road above. Plentiful seats line the pathway presenting lots of opportunities for sitting and enjoying the views. Occasional sheltered areas have been scooped out of the cliffs, providing welcome seating and respite from the wind on more bracing days.

As this path terminates, several routes can be taken either up onto the higher lawns, down to the beach or into the 'secret' garden that is something of a hidden gem. Originally an old chalk pit, the Italian Gardens were landscaped in 1904 and once the steep descent has been made, one has the sense of being enveloped in a green wooded amphitheatre. It is appropriate therefore that in the summer months the gardens play host to a series of very popular open-air performances. Perhaps not surprisingly, Shakespeare's *A Midsummer Night's Dream* is always a favourite when staged in this setting.

It is nice to take the return journey back to the town centre along the lower promenade. Set amid long elevated strips of more mixed planting are several rustic summer houses providing shelter from the sun, wind or rain, depending on the time of year. These are splendid, if slightly incongruous structures, with their thatched roofs, ornate timbering and decorative brickwork. They naturally conjure up scenes of an all together more bucolic setting rather than the view they afford of sea, sand (well, more often pebbles) and bathers. However, it is just this unusually close juxtaposition of planting and sea that makes a visit to Eastbourne Seafront Gardens so enjoyable.

**Getting there**                                        National grid ref. TU61980
- Eastbourne, East Sussex.
- Eastbourne Borough Council, tel 01323 410000, website: www.eastbourne.gov.uk
- Buses to Eastbourne. Ten minutes walk from Eastbourne Station.
- **Other gardens nearby:** Alfriston Clergy House (see *page 25*), Michelham Priory (see *page 56*) Herstmonceaux Castle.

# GREAT DIXTER

## NORTHIAM

D ue to the energetic creativity and imagination of the late
plantsman, gardener and writer Christopher Lloyd (*1921-
2006*) Great Dixter has become one of the most famous and
influential gardens in England over recent years. No matter during which
season you visit, there is always something inspiring and innovative to
stimulate the senses. The Great Dixter Charitable Trust was founded
shortly before Lloyd's death to enable the house and garden to continue
to enchant and delight future visitors. The garden is in the very safe
hands of Fergus Garrett, who has been head gardener for many years,
and his team. Garrett and Lloyd worked side by side to create one of
the late 20th- century's most dynamic gardens.

The settled and established appearance of the house somewhat belies
its true origins, indeed only one portion of the house was originally
built *in situ* in the 15th century. An early 16th-century yeoman's house
from Benenden in Kent was dismantled and re-erected here in 1910
with new additions completed two years later. It was at this point that
the substantially enlarged Dixter house gained the Great in its name.
This ambitious programme of development began when Nathaniel Lloyd
purchased the property in 1910 and engaged the architect Edwin Lutyens
(*1869-1944*). Both men were keen that whatever changes were made
to the original house should be in harmony with the local vernacular; the
Benenden timber-framed house was acquired at Lutyens' suggestion.

Lloyd died in 1933 and the house and estate continued to be run by his widow Daisy. On her death in 1972 her son Christopher took over the complete running of the house, nursery and gardens. It is now possible to visit both house and garden or simply the garden alone.

The Dixter estate extends to 23 hectares but no garden existed in 1910, only a few trees. Some, such as the still fruiting 'William' pears, have survived. Nathaniel Lloyd established much of the architectural framework of the garden that exists today, including the yew hedges and some of the topiary, a particular interest of his. His book *Topiary: Garden Craftsmanship in Yew and Box* is still in print. Lutyens worked extensively on the design of the garden creating a layout that is both sympathetic to the agricultural heritage of the site (existing farm buildings were adapted and put to new use) and aesthetically appropriate to the remodelled house.

The approach up the path to the house takes the visitor through an area of meadow, enclosed by yew hedging with a view to the rather alarmingly leaning timbered porch. Only the variety and exuberance of the flower pots that cluster round the entrance porch give any indication of the joyous colour that lies within. The tapestry-like areas of meadow grass at Great Dixter are rightly famous and have done much to promote the popularity of this style of cultivation. Those to the front of the house are probably at their most beautiful in spring. It was Christopher Lloyd's mother who initially introduced the meadows to the garden; she painstakingly raised wild daffodils and snakeshead fritillaries from seed and individually transplanted them into the meadow grass. Lloyd went on to develop the meadows and experiment with introductions of native and foreign species.

To the right of the house lies the Sunk Garden. Having been turned over to vegetables in World War I by Nathaniel Lloyd, the area was later excavated and the octagonal pond placed at its centre. The higher level is known as the Barn Garden and 'Brunswick' figs (as stipulated by Lutyens) grow against one of the barn walls. Here, as everywhere else at Great Dixter, one is aware of the irregularly shaped skyline formed from the sheltering presence of roofs, chimneys, oast-house cowls, topiary or hedges.

One of the pleasures gained by a visit to Great Dixter is the real sense of this being a private garden developed and tended by a loving owner over a long period of time. Personal touches, such as the pebble mosaic (designed by Miles Johnson and executed by Maggie Howarth and Mark Davidson) of Lloyd's much-loved dachshunds, the appropriately named Dahlia and Canna, abound. Note how the tips of paws and tails just nudge out of the main design into the York stone-paving surround. Likewise the large grouping of imaginatively planted pots, alongside the mosaic in the Wall Garden, help create a sense of intimacy and care so often missing from large-scale gardens that are inevitably tended by non-resident gardeners.

To the rear of the house can be found the loggia which looks out over the Topiary Lawn, again with varied skyline of roofs and chimneys beyond. Tile ends form the eight sturdy pillars of the structure, a decorative technique that Lutyens typically deployed elsewhere in the garden, notably on arches and steps. More of Lutyens' work can be found in the Topiary Garden. The timber seat is his design; another has been used to terminate the vista at the end of the Long Border (both are now replicas of the originals).

The Long Border is a triumph of successional planting flowering from April to October, although it reaches its zenith from mid-June to mid-August. Lloyd often said that he strove to achieve the effect of 'a closely woven tapestry' and certainly no bare earth can be seen, only a rich mixture of colour, form and texture. This is very much a mixed border rather than the herbaceous kind; shrubs rub shoulders with annuals, perennials and climbers. The spirit of so much of the planting at Great Dixter is about breaking or extending traditionally accepted rules and creating new ways of looking at and arranging things. Tall plants that allow sufficient views through them to the things behind are placed at the front of borders not only at the back. Similarly daring or unlikely colour combinations are tried and tested. Self-seeders proliferate and are often the authors of pleasant and unexpected arrangements.

From the Long Border and terrace an unusual configuration of Lutyens-designed circular steps descends to the Orchard below (the scene of long-flowering daffodils from March to May). Beds are set within the steps and have been planted with cacti and agaves. These Mediterranean-style beds act as something of a preparation and intro-duction to what lies beyond. The Exotic Garden was originally a rose garden but now buzzes in summer with a heady mix of heat and colour more readily associated with the tropics than an English country garden. Bounded on three sides by tall yew hedges and a low barn on the fourth, the space is an enclosed oasis of colour and scent. The open barn, known as The Hovel, provides welcome shade from the heat, both real and atmospheric, outside. If riotous-coloured dahlias, swaying bamboos, bold cannas and heavy-leaved banana plants are now a more common sight in private and public gardens than before, then the inspiration for the trend can be found here.

The High Garden is the original Edwardian kitchen garden for the house and the traditional form of the cruciform paths can still be seen. It now houses stock for the garden and nursery as well as some fruit and vegetables. Next to the High Garden is the Peacock Topiary Garden in which densely planted beds are punctuated with the structural form of 18 giant birds.

Great Dixter is unique. The gardens wrap themselves around a very special house that provides the classic English backdrop of generous tiled roofs and sheltering eaves. This, along with the topiary, is enlivened by the characteristically exuberant Lloyd planting displaying often radical and unexpected colour combinations. However, such richness comes at a price and this is high-maintenance gardening par excellence which can only be achieved with a small army of talented gardeners. If you visit and your passions are stirred then why not become a Friend of Great Dixter and help support the Charitable Trust to preserve and nurture the spirit of the house and garden for the future.

**Getting there**                                    National grid ref. TQ818250

- Northiam, Nr. Rye, East Sussex, TN31 6PH.
- The Great Dixter Charitable Trust, tel 01797 252878, website: www.greatdixter.co.uk
- South of Tenterden on the A28.
- **Other gardens nearby:** Lamb House, Merriments Garden (*see page 53*), Pashley Manor Gardens.

# HIGHDOWN GARDENS

## WORTHING

If any gardener is daunted at the prospect of establishing a new garden on a patch of uninviting chalky soil, then a visit to Highdown Gardens should more than allay their fears. The garden was begun in 1909 by the distinguished soldier and biologist Sir Frederick Stern (*1884-1967*) and his wife Sybil on the singularly unpromising site of an old chalk pit. Here they worked for 50 years and created a unique garden of great interest which sits harmoniously with its downland backdrop and seaward views. The Sterns occupied Highdown Towers, originally built in *c.*1820, until Sir Frederick's death in 1967, when his widow handed both the house and the garden over to Worthing Borough Council. The house is now a hotel.

Stern bought the house and land in 1909 and although he didn't take up residence immediately, work started on the garden at once. The rock garden and round pond were completed by 1910 but it was not until his marriage to Sybil in 1919 that he settled here and work on the garden began in earnest. Sir Frederick published a detailed account of the making of Highdown, *A Chalk Garden*, in 1960 and it still offers invaluable advice to anyone gardening on chalk. It is something of an antidote to the glossy modern-day gardening book, with its scholarly and detailed exposition of the growing habits and performance of many individual species. However, occasionally his writing can be quite evocative such as when describing *Tulip kaufmanniana*.

*On sunny mornings when the flowers open wide showing their light yellow*
*petals, they remind one of the young blackbirds in the nests with their beaks wide*
*open waiting for their mother to come home with food.*[1]

Stern's ethos was one of experimentation tempered by patient trial and
error. He strove to find plants that settled and thrived in these very
particular soil conditions and in the exposed coastal climate. However,
the conditions across the garden are far from uniform, thus a wide
number of species grow happily. Also pockets of acid soil have been
introduced to enable plants such as heathers and camellias to grow here
too. The garden is exposed to salt-laden southerly winds and the elm
shelterbelt so wisely planted by Stern was lost to the double depriva-
tions of Dutch elm disease and the 1987 storm. Replacement planting
of ash, pine and ilex oak is underway on the western side of the site.

Highdown boasts an impressive range of plants, many originally
grown from small specimens or seeds brought back from expeditions
by plant hunters such as Frank Kingdon-Ward and Ernest Henry Wilson
(Stern dedicated his book on chalk gardening to the latter). Stern also
subscribed to the 1914 China expedition to Yunnan and Kansu by
Reginald Farrer. Magnolias, wisterias, lilies, rhododendrons and azaleas
were all introduced into the garden from stock that originated in far-
flung places, including a Judas tree (*Cercis siliquastrum*) originally grown
from seed from Afghanistan. Sir Frederick also raised a number of plants
at Highdown, most famously Rosa 'Highdownensis,' 1928 and the rose
'Wedding Day', 1950, which originally first flowered on the Stern's
wedding anniversary, hence its name. He seductively described it thus,

*It is a very strong climber and has now completely covered a cherry tree; the*
*flowers make a mass over the whole plant, buds being apricot, opening pure white*
*and dying pink with stems bronze.*[2]

Stern also contributed much to the revival of interest in growing lilies,
founding the Lily Group of the Royal Horticultural Society. He gained

1. Stern, F.C., The Chalk Garden, *Faber & Faber, London, 1974, p.38.*
2. *Ibid, p.108.*

his knighthood in 1956 for Services to Horticulture. Highdown is now home to the National Collection, 'The Plant Introductions of Sir Frederick Stern, administered by the National Council for the Conservation of Plants and Gardens'. Any remaining gaps in the collection of plants lost are gradually being filled.

Highdown has many areas, including a small herb garden, cherry avenue, hellebore bank, rose garden and beech wood. Each month brings new interest. Late winter and early spring boasts wonderful displays of naturalised snowdrops, crocus, daffodils, anemones and hellebores (forming a multi-coloured display on the extensive Hellebore Bank), giving way in May to splendid tree peonies. Then day lilies and bearded iris steal the show as summer advances, followed by philadelphus and agapanthus.

The tree and shrub area lies just beyond the garden entrance and was ploughed up in World War II as they did their bit producing vegetables for the Dig For Victory campaign. Viburnum, cotoneaster, sorbus and euonymus now flourish there. Below lies a lovely shaded walk planted with Himalayan Birch Bark Cherries on one side and roses on the other. A small-scale fenced Millennium Garden was made to celebrate the new century funded by generous donations made to Highdown and has a cool white, blue and green colour theme. Complete with small pool, sundial and meandering paths, low mixed beds surround a shaded seat. Here the emphasis is on water conservation, with an underground watering system and labour-saving devices such as wood and bark mulches, so is of special interest to those gardening domestically on dry chalky soil.

Wandering into the Chalk Pit Garden is a little like entering a high-sided theatrical arena. From the expanse of lawn the sides of the original chalk pit are now completely clothed in a wide variety of shrubs and plants. It is hard to imagine that the vast range of shape, form and colour one now sees must once have appeared as a stark white scar on the landscape as the chalk was excavated and used to lime surrounding fields. Now exotic introductions sit happily next to native and more common species. The two ponds at Highdown are in this area, the Cave Pond was created on the site of an old lime kiln. Here chalk was burnt to make quicklime, probably in the 17th and 18th centuries. An attractive rockery of Horsham stone, designed by Clarence Elliot, surrounds the water's edge. This is a magical place with a deep curvaceous pool receding deep into the rocks at the rear. A cleverly tiered waterfall provides the gentle sound of trickling water and a giant clump of towering arum lilies rises from the centre of the main pool. As its name suggests, the nearby Bamboo Pond is backed by a rampant clump of bamboo (*Arundinaria nitida*) planted *c.* 1910.

On the higher ground above the Cave Pond is the Rose Garden. Island beds contain roses of all habits including climbers, shrubs and ramblers, interplanted with hardy geraniums. A rose-smothered pergola divides this area and further roses are found down the steps. The Middle Garden boasts a Chinese weeping hornbeam (*Carpinus turczaninowii*) planted by Queen Mary in 1937 while she was a guest of the Sterns. Yet another venerable Sussex tree to suffer in the Great Storm of 1987 was Highdown's Strawberry tree (*Arbutus x andrachnoides*) originally from Hilliers in 1924. The whole tree was uprooted but the replanting of a healthy side shoot survived and is now flourishing. Over 100 trees in total were lost at Highdown on that terrible night. Raised ericaceous beds house camellias and rhododendrons. Along the southern boundary the very long Rose Pergola has been restored and supports many of the old cultivars that were firm Stern favourites.

Highdown has been the worthy winner of more than one Green Flag Award for Public Parks. This is a Nationwide Award Scheme for Parks and Gardens that promotes environmentally-friendly policies such as the banning of the use of peat and the implementation of green waste recycling. The staff at Highdown are firmly committed to the scheme, along with welcoming and informing their many visitors. All this and there is no admission charge to the garden!

**Getting there** National grid ref. TQ095042
- Littlehampton Road, Worthing, West Sussex, BN12 6PE.
- Worthing Borough Council, tel 01903 501054, website: www.highdowngardens.co.uk
- West of Worthing on the A259.
- **Other gardens nearby:** Arundel Castle, Denmans Garden (*see page 28*).

# KIPLING GARDENS

## ROTTINGDEAN

The Kipling Gardens are idyllically situated on Rottingdean's picturesque village green. The site of the green, with its lovely natural pond, has been the focal point for local inhabitants since Saxon times. Shepherds regularly herded their flocks to drink at the pond until the advance of the motor vehicle made this untenable. The gardens occupy what was once part of the common land of the green so it is particularly fitting that this place of peace and beauty is now open to everyone, everyday and for free!

This area of the green merged with the grounds of the neighbouring property The Elms (now sadly lacking its eponymous trees) and became part of its garden. The 18th-century house was once the home of the author Rudyard Kipling (*1865-1936*) who rented it for three guineas a week from 1897 to 1902. Kipling knew the village well as his aunt, Georgina Burne-Jones, owned North End House and holidayed there with her husband the Pre-Raphaelite painter Sir Edward Burne-Jones (the artist William Nicholson and later Enid Bagnold, author of *National Velvet*, were also to live there). The nearby St Margaret's Church has some fine Morris & Co. stained glass designed by Burne-Jones. Kipling wrote many of his *Just So Stories* here but the idyll was not to last. The desolation he felt at the death of his daughter Josephine was compounded by his lack of privacy. Kipling suffered an early manifestation of celebrity stalking when the landlord of the White Horse Hotel began to organise horse-drawn double decker bus tours from Brighton. These toured the village and drove close alongside the walls of The Elms, providing uninterrupted views into the garden. This hastened Kipling's move to Bateman's (*see p.12*), a house less exposed to prying eyes.

In the early 1980s almost a hectare of The Elms' garden was divided off and a planning application submitted to build houses there. The Rottingdean Preservation Society vigorously opposed the plan and eventually triumphed. With the aid of active fundraising and a generous bequest, the Society was able to purchase the site and spent three years renovating the walls and paths and establishing the bones of the garden we see today. The gardens were handed over to the local authority in 1986 and are now so beautifully maintained by Brighton & Hove City Council that some lines from Kipling's 1911 poem *The Glory of the Garden* seem particularly apt.

> Our England is a garden, and such gardens are not made
> By singing:- 'Oh, how beautiful,' and sitting in the shade,
> While better men than we go out and start their working lives
> At grubbing weeds from gravel-paths with broken dinner-knives.

The gardens should be entered from the green, just north of the pond. One immediate dilemma the visitor is presented with is to choose where to sit, as so many lovely sheltered seats are furnished for their use. The gardens are divided into about half a dozen areas, each flowing seamlessly one to another. The first space one enters has an attractive Arts and Crafts-style covered gazebo, while a bench in the sun offers a view of the interesting and varied elevation of North End House. For those with an interest in vernacular building methods the walls surrounding the gardens repay close study. A seemingly infinite variety of effects, using a combination of brick and flint, have been deployed in the building of these walls. Fine steps, buttresses and arches also add interest while oval 'windows' puncture the internal walls.

The large Rose Garden provides a mass of flower-filled beds, brimming with colour, scent and enviably disease-free blooms. Climbers take full advantage of the towering walls. The sturdy circular flint supports of the pergola also offer a robust framework for a range of climbing plants. An unusually shaped oval herb bed bakes in a sunny southerly spot and encloses an area of lawn with a centrally placed tree.

Tucked into the north east corner of the gardens is a beautifully tended croquet lawn, the only formal one in the city. It is slightly sunk down into the site and surrounded by sheltering herbaceous beds. More welcoming seats are provided for spectators and if play is slow the view to the horizon is a more than adequate diversion, as silhouetted against the sky is the omnipresent form of the Rottingdean Windmill, dating back to *c*.1802.

You leave the gardens via an enclosed woodland area to the north, which is especially delightful in spring with its underplanting of seasonal bulbs. A few picnic benches have been thoughtfully provided and certainly tea, cucumber sandwiches and cake here would be a fitting way to crown a visit to a garden so resonant with Edwardian associations. It may be something of a cliché but the Kipling Gardens do provide an oasis of calm from the mismanaged traffic that forms a tight girdle around the interior of this lovely village. Had it not been for the determination and energy of local residents these lovely gardens could so easily have been lost to the bulldozer. Do please repay their efforts by a visit; I can promise you won't regret it.

**Getting there**                                   National grid ref. TQ369027

- Village Green, Rottingdean, East Sussex, BN2 7HA.
- Brighton & Hove City Council, tel 01273 290000, website: www.brighton-hove.gov.uk
- Frequent buses along the coast road to Rottingdean both from the direction of Brighton and Eastbourne.
- **Other gardens nearby:** Preston Park (see *page 72*), Pavilion Gardens.

# LEONARDSLEE GARDENS

## LOWER BEEDING

In many ways a trip to Leonardslee is quite unlike visiting any of the other gardens featured in this book. It is far more like going on a beautiful woodland walk than strolling round a garden, although in country that resembles visions of a selectively planted Himalayan Eden rather than the more ubiquitous scenes of Sussex. If one then adds to this heightened sense of entering an idyll the occasional glimpse of springing wallabies (yes, real marsupials!) all comparisons with other gardens fail completely.

The gardens were begun in 1801 by the Beauclerk family. They were followed by the Hubbards who demolished the existing house and erected the present one in 1855, designed by the architect Thomas Donaldson. Sir Edmund Loder married into the Hubbard family and bought the estate from his in-laws in 1889. An enthusiastic gardener, with a particular penchant for exotic plants, he developed the gardens extensively. The gardens were opened to the public in 1907, originally for just a few days in spring. However, such is their popularity that over the years this has increased to daily between spring and autumn. Today the gardens are still owned and maintained by the Loder family.

The entrance is through a large greenhouse, the home to tropical palms, bananas and agaves. The original Loder home is still in evidence but is now in private use and not part of the gardens. Other buildings within the grounds have been utilised for the usual facilities along with a collection of the family's Victorian motor cars and a miniature estate village. An award-winning display of bonsai is on view in an open court-yard and for the enthusiast the Alpine House boasts a large collection of the species but it rather lacks atmosphere or aesthetic appeal. However, the real interest of this garden lies beyond these initial attractions and I suggest that you wander into the real heart of the place promptly. Once on the Terrace looking down to the wonderful views of the wooded valley below, the noise of the traffic is replaced by that of birdsong.

The original layout and planting owes much to the picturesque move-ment, although some of the wilder aspects of the style have been tempered by the use of exotic-looking species rather than craggy and irregular trees and shrubs. The damp and acidic soil so characteristic of this valley provides the perfect growing conditions for rhododendrons, camellias, azaleas and magnolias. The hybrid *Rhododendron x 'Loderi'* is named after Loder and the original stock is still in the garden. Spring and early summer are particularly stunning at Leonardslee. Later in the season great clumps of hydrangeas steal the show before the tints of autumn begin to appear. For colour, autumn easily rivals spring once the maples come into their own.

Although the gardens are vast, 97 hectares in all, I think that the best way to enjoy them is to throw away the helpfully provided map and just walk as the fancy takes you. Your wanderings will lead you into the Dell. This is a magical place, tropical in feel, full of tree ferns and enormous gunneras, punctuated by tall pines and conifers. The sounds and smells that emanate from deep within this woodland are all-pervasive, the best way I can describe it is a little like being in a 'dry rainforest.' A clearing in the Dell reveals a memorial table to Edmund G. Loder who 'made and loved these gardens'. Sit by the table and look down to the lakes below. Appreciate the skilful and mature planting, the rich and varied textures of the multitude of trees and shrubs. The beautiful series of seven lakes which lies at the bottom of the valley has a surprisingly util-itarian origin as they were dug to provide waterpower for the iron industry. Now they add tranquillity to the garden and act as a mirror to reflect the lovely planting all around.

Both in terms of fauna and flora, not all is large and exotic at Leonardslee and there is ample room for the small and humble. Wild flowers thrive here. Spring brings wonderful displays of naturalised cowslips, primroses and bluebells. Variously scattered around the grounds and left undisturbed are a large variety of wildflowers including bugle, orpine, yarrow, musk mallow, meadowsweet and heathers. The list seems almost inexhaustible. Natural and native wildlife also abound and the visitor has the opportunity to study the more common or garden types such as butterflies, squirrels, rabbits and a variety of wildfowl (although the black swans on the lakes do add an irresistible air of glamour).

The Rock Garden lies on the higher ground of the garden just beyond the greenhouse and the exterior gives no indication of the scale within. The visitor enters a wonderful space intersected by paths that climb up and down through dense evergreen planting. Great slabs of tiered rocks create irregular forms from which grow an abundance of plants. James Pulham (junior) was employed by Sir Edmund to create the garden using a mixture of natural and artificial sandstone. Pulham was also responsible for the rock enclosure originally built for Loder's mouflon and mountain sheep, now utilised as breeding pens for the wallabies.

Sir Edmund's enthusiasm for the exotic embraced the animal kingdom as well as plants. The wallabies were an 1889 import of his and their subsequent popularity with successive generations of Loders may in part be due to their efficient, and eco-friendly, performance as lawn mowers. The estate was also home to antelopes, beavers and kangaroos in his time. Today the extensive parkland provides further acres for walking, with the added chance of seeing the resident herds of sika, fallow and axis deer, but sadly no antelopes! Presently closed, consult the website.

**Getting there**                                        National grid ref. TQ221262
 ❯ Lower Beeding, near Horsham, West Sussex, RH13 6PP.
 ❯ Website: www.leonardsleegardens.co.uk
 ❯ On the A281, nearest station Horsham five miles (eight kilometres), buses from Brighton
   and Horsham.
 ❯ **Other gardens nearby;** Nymans Gardens (see page 59), Sylvia Standing Garden
   (see page 79).

# MARCHANTS HARDY PLANTS

## LAUGHTON

Marchants Hardy Plants is the most recently made garden featured in this book and certainly lacks nothing of the creative energy and innovation so readily associated with Bright Young Things. If ever one feels jaded and jaundiced with looking at gardens (or indeed at life) then a visit to Marchants will swiftly administer an invigorating cure.

What is now an oasis of colour, texture and movement was simply a wind-swept field when Graham Gough and Lucy Goffin moved here in 1998. The whole garden benefits from the dramatic and beautiful view of the ridge of Downs to the south. However, such an auspicious setting came at a price as the soil in this particular corner of Sussex is heavy clay. Graham has (manually) added 100 tonnes of spent mushroom compost and the equivalent in grit to improve on nature's rather mean bequest. The site is modest in size, less than a hectare, and is long. Its widest point is to the north, where the garden narrows as it gradually progresses away from the entrance. Sinuous paths and soft undulations in ground level lead you towards the landscape beyond. Trees are used imaginatively throughout and the southern end has the beginnings of a pond. Here also is an enclosed wild garden, a haven for animal as well as plant life. Marchants is a garden with very long seasonal interest, providing the visitor with excitement and delight from the earliest bulbs to late autumn colour.

Apart from the condition of the soil another challenge initially facing the intrepid makers of this garden was how to shelter and establish plants in such an exposed site while waiting for hedges and screens to grow. This is a problem faced by many gardeners in Sussex, a county that has its fair share of windy coastline, valleys and hilltops. While many of us reach for the effective but aesthetically unpleasing green nylon netting this creative pair found an altogether more innovative and lyrical solution. Needing to find a permeable screen which allowed the air to be filtered rather than deflected (wind simply whips over a solid structure, such as a wall, and still blasts the plants behind) Graham erected a series of slatted fences, ingeniously constructed from tannalised roof battens. Rather than trim them to a consistent height he took inspiration from the line of the Downs beyond and cut them into gentle undulating shapes, creating a visual echo of what Kipling called the 'blunt, bow-headed whale-backed Downs'.

Marchants is not just a garden but also a nursery and Graham raises and grows only the finest and best. His planting is modern but never faddy, innovative but lacking whimsicality. All the plants here have to earn their place in this well-edited garden and only the fittest (both in effect and performance) make the grade. One of the signatures of Graham's planting style is his clever use of ornamental grasses. This group of plants has perhaps rather suffered in recent years, first enjoying a rapid rise in popularity and fashion, then often failing to create the desired effect when grown by the average gardener. They can be difficult to incorporate into existing planting schemes and have too often failed to make the transition successfully from garden centre or nursery to the domestic flower bed in the back garden. This is a great shame as there are so many varied forms, sizes, textures and colours and all can add a new and exciting dimension to the mixed border. Certainly, anyone who has ever been sniffy about or dismissive of the good old pampas grass should take a look at the stunning variegated golden one grown here, then think again! The gardens at nearby Glyndebourne are another excellent example of the harmonious mixing of this group of plants within a primarily herbaceous structure. If successful integration of grasses has so far evaded you, fear not, come to Marchants and see how it should be done.

Two of the real sensual contributions to be made to a garden by members of the grass family are movement and sound. The beds at Marchants shimmer and sway, then rustle and hiss in the breeze. Added to this is the urge to stroke the grasses as you pass as so many evoke tactile associations with fur and feather. Set amid the relative subtlety of the form and hue of these grasses sings the vibrant colours of a huge range of herbaceous perennials. Achilleas, agapanthus, alliums, crocosmias, echinaceas, kniphofias, perovskias and verbenas. These are just a few of the dazzling patches of colour that appear throughout the planting here. Marchants also has much to teach us about scale. As at Great Dixter (*see p. 35*) tall plants are not just relegated to the back of the border but are encouraged to spill over paths and create tall 'tunnels' for the visitor to walk through. However, do not expect rampant abandon – there is no anarchy at Marchants, as each plant has its carefully allotted place and territory.

Graham and Lucy's arrangement of individual plants shows a considered and skilful appreciation of their varying form, texture and colour, a result that must owe much to Lucy's long experience as a leading textile designer. Their layering of one plant against another, along with their overall consideration of shape, has created a sense of depth and recession within the garden which belies the relatively small scale of the overall site. One very much stands within the garden at Marchants, rather than surveys its entirety, unaware of quite where its boundaries lie. Much of the layout comprises interlocking circles and curves. Small elevated mounds have been created and add yet another dimension to the visitor's progression through the garden: one is up high and then takes a shallow descent down into an enclosure sheltered on all sides by plants; turn a corner and you are hidden from the rest of the garden only to appear in a clearing again. This adds a subtle drama to the garden but one that is gradual and gentle, never startling.

For me Marchants has the sense that it has grown out of its very particular site and location in a completely natural and appropriate way, far more than most Sussex gardens I have visited. The arrangement of plants sits happily at ease with its characteristic downland backdrop, always enhancing rather than detracting. This is nothing short of miraculous considering the age of the garden. Perhaps, one of its talented makers should have the last word.

> *Our lives and our philosophy of living, as regards both work and pleasure,*
> *are now inextricably linked to the elements and the landscape that surround*
> *us here at Marchants and, constantly humbled by the presence of the ancient*
> *and timeless Downs, we reflect on what is, in the greater scheme of things,*
> *our brief curatorship of this small plot of earth.* [1]

1. *Gough, Graham*, The Best Teacher a Gardener Can Have, *Hortus, No 69, Spring 2004, p38.*

**Getting there**    National grid ref. TQ510124
- 2, Marchants Cottages, Mill Lane, Laughton, East Sussex, BN8 6AJ.
- Graham Gough and Lucy Goffin, tel 01323 811737, website: www.marchantshardyplants.co.uk
- Just south of the B2124.
- **Other gardens nearby:** Alfriston Clergy House (see page 25), Charleston Farmhouse (see page 21), Michelham Priory (see page 56), Monk's House (see page 23).

# MERRIMENTS GARDEN

## HURST GREEN

Until as recently as the early 1990s the horticultural wonder now known as Merriments Garden was simply an old farm field with a boggy centre. Today it is a superb example of a well-planned and designed inspiring garden space which has much to teach all who visit. Despite its size (1.6 hectares) and ambition the joy of Merriments lies in the clever way the space has been skilfully divided into various areas, each with its own particular mood and growing conditions. For the new gardener each of these distinct spaces can act as a template to copy and adapt to the smaller-scale domestic garden (clear labelling of individual plants also helps make this feasible). But please do not think of Merriments as falling prey to that rather worn cliché of the 'garden room'. The divisions here, where they do occur, are subtle; each area ebbs and flows into the other without interruption or barrier.

At Merriments wide sinuous beds are divided by generous and beautifully tended lawns. Indeed every inch of the ground here is so immaculately kept that I'm sure a 'hunt the weed' competition would yield few winners! Varied trees of many shapes and sizes have been incorporated into the deep beds and, along with the various pots and sculptures, act as focal points giving a sense of scale to the planting below. If I have any criticism of this garden it is perhaps the overly ubiquitous use of these pots and sculptures. While inevitably some are more successful than others, the frequency at which they occur does result in some of their impact being lost. A slight feeling of the shop display is apparent here and there: with garden ornament, the rule usually is less is definitely more.

A central pond forms the focal heart of the garden. From the viewing deck the various habitats can be studied, including the running stream and the boggy areas, all framed by a lovely overhanging willow tree. This main pond feeds a smaller one in the Tropical Garden. A red oriental-style bridge, reminiscent of the one at Monet's Giverny, takes you across the water to a wilder, more natural area. In spring the trees here are under-planted with flowering bulbs. An intriguing 'living hut' has been constructed by planting an almost complete circle of beech hedging. This has grown high and is being trained to form a roof. The igloo-shaped hut is green in summer and brown in spring and autumn and is very inviting, especially to children.

Close by is a specially designed wildlife habitat complete with various bird feeders, a small pond for newts, toads and frogs and a pile of bark and logs to encourage insects and small mammals. Weasels have also been spotted here. A sensitively constructed covered viewing station allows you to observe the multitude of visiting birds and wildlife in all weathers and without fear of detection. This delightful area also houses a traditional beehive, complete with resident swarm, and looks partic-ularly fitting in this environment.

An uncompromising shingle and gravel garden introduces a sharp change in mood. Set among the blue gravel are various grasses and verbe-nas, many no doubt self-seeders. Stately agaves planted in pots complete the Mediterranean feel. Alongside this area is a lovely grove of silver birch trees, a scaled down version of which would work perfectly in a larger than average domestic garden. Anyone with a garden that is much longer than it is wide could incorporate this at the end of their plot to blur the boundary and add a sense of depth and mystery.

The Bog Garden is wittily graced by an old gate, which is gradually being consumed by the wide variety of plants that thrive in these damp conditions. Tall stately bamboos and old tree stumps lend this area a slightly eccentric air recalling the Victorian fashion of the stumpery.

The only fully contained area within Merriments is the large formal garden. It is approached through wide spanning arches and is enclosed by walls and hedges. A central rill is the focal point of the space while surrounding box is clipped into low hedges and pyramids. Japanese barberry (*thunbergii 'Atropurpurea'*) has also been used as a low-growing hedge and provides a dramatic and very attractive colour contrast to the dark green of the box. The beds are stylishly planted with blocks of white and burgundy tulips in spring, along with forget-me-nots and narcissi. These are followed later in the year by alliums, pinks, anthemis, diasca, asters and roses. A bed planted with various herbs provides a carpet of scent and colour around a classical stone urn. This formal space is in sharp contrast to the more meandering feel of the rest of the garden and consequently has great impact.

The lack of an historical context at Merriments has encouraged its makers to be particularly free and experimental with ideas. For instance a very new take on a very old form – the pergola – has been constructed. Pairs of tall stout wooden poles that form an inverted V are repeated and stride along a path, providing support for scrambling climbers. Many of the borders are themed by colour. The Hot Borders are a riot of colour in late summer while the Golden Border shimmers with every conceivable shade and hue of yellow. An interesting and varied use of paths is deployed throughout the garden, again providing inspiration and instruction for the domestic gardener.

The exit from the garden is through the plant centre and nursery. Here a well-selected choice of plants is for sale, most of which can be seen growing in the garden. But be warned, after experiencing such an inspiring example of planting only the most steely willed or the most impoverished will be able to leave without an overflowing car boot!

---

**Getting there**          National grid ref. TQ738280

- Hawkhurst Road, Hurst Green, East Sussex, TN19 7RA.
- Merriments, tel 01580 860666, website: www.merriments.co.uk
- Southwest of Hawkhurst on the A229.
- Etchingham Station approximately one and a half miles (two and a half kilometres).
- **Other gardens nearby:** Bateman's (see *page 12*), Pashley Manor Gardens.

# MICHELHAM PRIORY

## UPPER DICKER

Michelham Priory must have one of the most romantic entrances of any garden in Sussex. Having approached the moated property by bridge and gatehouse, the visitor finds the 13th-century priory at the centre of a 3-hectare island, surrounded on all sides by delightfully landscaped grounds. The picturesque Augustinian priory was founded in 1229 by Gilbert de l'Aigle, the Norman Lord of Pevensey. It boasts the largest filled medieval moat in England and the surrounding water adds a timeless air of stillness and tranquillity.

The monastery took over a century to build and was endowed with extensive lands. However, the Black Death of 1349 drastically reduced the number of canons to a mere five; there would never be more than 10 in the years to come. This resulted in the priory having to struggle to offer the level of hospitality expected by passing nobles, pilgrims and travellers. In 1537 Michelham fell prey to the vandalism of Henry VIII's dissolution of the monasteries, resulting in the church and several buildings on the site being demolished.

The Priory then had something of a chequered history with many owners and much of the land divided and disposed of. Thomas, Lord de la Warr undertook some restoration of the main buildings in the 16th century then in 1601 Thomas Sackville, Lord Buckhurst purchased the property. Although it remained in the Sackville family for almost 300 years, it was always let to tenant farmers.

From the late 19th century onwards successive owners carried out restoration work to the priory but it was its post-war owner, Mrs Hotblack, who opened the historic site to visitors for the first time, developing the gardens and opening a restaurant. Mrs Hotblack later presented the Priory to its present owners, the Sussex Archaeological Society. The main house is open to the public and has a comprehensive and interesting display detailing the history of the site. The old barnyard houses several 19th- and 20th-century agricultural wagons and interesting paraphernalia. A fully restored and working 14th-century watermill is situated just beyond the moat and stone-ground wholemeal flour made from wheat ground at the mill can be purchased.

The beautifully tended gardens are a mix of the ancient and the more recent. The moat is thought to have been built towards the end of the 14th century, at the same time that the gatehouse was constructed. On the eastern corner of the island can be found an original stew pond. This would have been one of several ponds in which the canons stored fish netted from the moat or the nearby Cuckmere River. Pleasant wilderness and moat walks that follow the periphery of the moat can be enjoyed by crossing one of the two footbridges to the north and east. Here a lazy hour or two can be whiled away in the shade, picnicking and enjoying the views back across the moat to the priory.

Although appropriate to the history of the site the physic garden to the south of the house actually dates from 1981. Basking in full sun, the garden contains almost 100 varieties of plants, commonly used for medicinal and culinary purposes from medieval times to the present day. The plants are well identified with an explanation of their uses. Another area which has been developed more recently yet, and that is consistent with the spirit of the site, is the cloister garden. Constructed on the site of the original priory, it is cruciform in design. Medicinal or physic herbs, along with vegetables and ornamental plants are grown here. The atmosphere is calm, meditative and contemplative. If the weather is dry, do try the camomile seat!

The orchard area is also in keeping with the history of the Priory. Here the trees are underplanted with wild flowers and in the summer months serpentine paths are mown through the long grass. Like so many Sussex gardens, Michelham has sadly lost many of its trees both to Dutch elm disease and to the 1987 hurricane and an active programme of replanting has been undertaken.

Replanting has also reinvigorated the long herbaceous border which is a riot of colour and profusion of form from spring until late autumn. Behind this is one of the triumphs of the garden, the beautiful and productive organic kitchen garden. A formal tunnel intersects the space and is generously clothed with fruit and flowers and a sculpture of a bucolic female figure acts as a focal point. In summer the beds heave with a wide range of vegetables and flowers and the whole is surrounded by a sheltering hedge of clipped yew.

The most recent addition to the Michelham Priory garden is Les Jardins de Valloires. This is a friendship garden planted to celebrate the twinning of Michelham with this garden in the Somme region of northern France, devised as part of the EU 'Interreg' scheme. Michelham is also host to an Annual Garden Sculpture Trail which exploits to the full the site as a stunning setting for the work of local artists.

---

**Getting there**                                    National grid ref. TQ557095
- Upper Dicker, East Sussex, BN27 3QS.
- Sussex Archaeological Society, tel 01323 844224, website: www.sussexpast.co.uk
- Berwick Station two and a half miles (four kilometres).
- Limited bus service by Cuckmere Community Bus.
- **Other gardens nearby:** Alfriston Clergy House (see page 25), Charleston Farmhouse (see page 21), Monk's House (see page 23), Southover Grange, Wellingham Herb Garden.

# NYMANS GARDEN

## HANDCROSS

N ymans is one of the most visited and best-loved gardens in Sussex. The origins of what we see and enjoy today owe everything to the highly creative and horticulturally knowledgeable Messel family. It was German stockbroker Ludwig Messel (*1847-1915*) who in 1890 brought his large family to settle at Nymans, which was then an early 19th-century villa with 240 hectares. An Italianate tower and enormous conservatory (to house tender exotics) were then added by architect Ernest George. The radical landscaping of the site began five years later and was the beginnings of a very fruitful partnership between Messel and his head gardener James Comber.

When Ludwig's son Leonard inherited, the by then rather overblown Victorian pile at Nymans was not to his wife Maud's taste. She favoured a more romantic mood, rebuilding the house in a mock medieval style and introducing elements such as tapestries and dark oak Jacobean furniture. Her subtler sensibilities extended to the garden. She created a Rose Garden planted with old varieties and herbs (this underwent extensive renovation in the late 1980s and is once again planted with her favoured old varieties) and informally arranged spring bulbs under trees and shrubs. Meanwhile her husband gained considerable success exhibiting new strains of magnolias, rhododendrons and camellias at the Royal Horticultural Society. Their youngest son was the celebrated theatre designer Oliver Messel.

The 1930s were really the Golden Age for the gardens at Nymans, a period in which they were much visited and written about. However, the following decade brought an abrupt change: the war reduced the number of gardeners from a robust 11 to just three elderly 'ineligibles'. Then came the post-war winter of 1947 which was one of the most severe on record; open fires blazed day and night in an attempt to keep the house at Nymans habitable. On a February night fire broke out and flames quickly engulfed the house destroying all but the ruined walls you see today. The garden survived and continued to be supervised by the Messels' daughter Anne and the family restored and made habitable a portion of the remaining house.

In 1954 Nymans was given to the National Trust (one of the first major gardens it acquired) but Anne remained closely involved until the late 1980s. She and her husband occasionally stayed in the part of the house which her parents had restored. Perhaps somewhat ironically over time the ruined walls outside, now smothered in climbers such as roses and honeysuckle, have assumed an ever more romantic mood and one that would surely have met with the late Maud's approval. Parts of the house are now open to the public and show just what a convincing medieval reproduction this is!

The Pinetum lies to the north of the site and is planted with a huge variety of trees. The emphasis is very much on the perpendicular and the vastness of the area allows these impressive sentinel specimens to be viewed with maximum impact. Again the storm of 1987 claimed many victims at Nymans, approaching 500 trees came down, although mercifully the two giant redwoods survived. Little thinning had occurred for many years and, once the devastation was cleared, light and air rein-vigorated areas of the garden and new planting was undertaken in 1990. The delightful 1907 garden pavilion in the Pinetum was designed by Ludwig Messel's brother Alfred.

Like so many Sussex landowners Ludwig subscribed to the plant expeditions of the day, notably those of Ernest Henry Wilson. Wilson's popular introduction the pocket-handkerchief tree (*Davidia involucrata vilmoriniana*) has grown here since 1908 and today a delightful copse of them can be found enclosed by groupings of unusually shaped box at the eastern edge of the Pinetum. Messel also grew copious varieties of rhododendrons. The impressive Lime Avenue fringes the eastern boundary of the garden and provides views over the estate's parkland and woods below. Protruding into the landscape is the Prospect, a classically-inspired viewing platform which reveals the elevated nature of the garden at Nymans and would not look out of place in a Renaissance garden at the side of one of the great Italian lakes. Unfortunately a few minutes spent here also emphasises the twin modern-day blights of traffic and airplane noise.

The Heather Garden dates from Ludwig Messel's time. A testament to the soil, rhododendrons and heathers obviously thrive here, the latter grow in great luxuriant mounds in island beds. Set amid the heathers is a set of stone steps that lead up to a type of tree house construction, really more a viewing station, which gives an elevated view down to the lawn below and the pergola beyond. This long tunnel constructed of stone and massive timber pillars drips with wisteria. Messel got the idea from the 1903 Japanese Exhibition in London, from whence he also purchased the four stone Japanese lanterns placed at each corner of the Croquet Lawn. The pergola suffered in the 1987 storm but the new planting is now firmly established and is breathtaking in early summer. This pergola is a good demonstration of the considerable impact that such a long, luxuriously planted structure always makes (just as with Peto's pergola at West Dean). Alas, shorter, truncated tunnels never achieve the same drama.

To the north-east of the house is the Sunk Garden, a beautiful area which is loosely enclosed by camellias. The stone loggia was built in the 1920s but appears to be much more ancient and this, along with the Istrian marble urn which forms the centrepiece of the garden, would not look out of place in one of the great Italian Renaissance gardens. The formally arranged bedding strikes a perfect balance between restraint and colour.

The semi-ruined house lies at the centre of the garden providing a unique and theatrical focal point, overseen by a superb huge Cedar of

Lebanon. The architectural forms of large clipped yew further add to the irregular skyline of the roofless structure. Clouds are glimpsed through glassless windows and roses clamber through and around the stone transoms. Hidden behind walls and yew lies the Forecourt. This charming walled garden with dovecote was restored in the mid-1960s using photographs from a 1932 *Country Life* article (another example of a garden restoration project that owes so much to this invaluable mine of information). This is an exceedingly well designed area that fits to perfection the house behind. A rare harmony has been achieved and the result is peaceful and calming.

By contrast, the Wall Garden raises the pulse somewhat! It is a theatrical triumph with a strong axial double herbaceous border dissecting the enclosed area. Ludwig Messel chose this sheltered area, formerly an orchard, in which to grow tender exotics. The Edwardian enthusiasm for formal Italian gardens is further in evidence here. The main vista terminates in a brick arch elaborately topped with decorative swags and cherubs. Where the paths meet is a fine fountain of Verona red marble cornered by large yew columns with heraldic-looking globes. The herbaceous border is immaculately conceived and tended, the yew and grass edging acting as perfect foils to its dazzling colour. Beyond the borders lie calmer areas of trees and shrubs, many of South American origin.

Sadly but probably inevitably Nymans suffers from the fate of so many other large and popular gardens that to some extent become victims of their own success. The logistics of managing increasing numbers of visitors has forced owners, in this case the National Trust, to reroute arriving visitors away from the original approach to the property. This inevitably leads to some of the initial impact of house and approach being lost; too often the visitor 'comes upon' the property amid the garden, rather than experiences the grand revelation so often carefully orchestrated by architect or garden designer. Other instances that come to mind are Petworth (*see p. 68*), Bateman's (*see p. 12*) and West Dean Gardens (*see p. 82*), all having now lost their original approaches. Again and again the visitor's first impression of a grand house and garden is the tearoom, toilets and shop! I fully appreciate that this is an evil born of necessity and is in large part caused by the need for adequate, and indeed ever-increasing, car parking, but it is a shame.

The house at Nymans is reached by a lovely, if circuitous, route, and as a result it very much feels buried within the garden. One more or less experiences the grounds 'back to front,' seeing first the landscaped and open aspects and then the more formal elements close to the house, such as the Wall and Rose Gardens, only later. Thus one loses the progression from house out through the most structured parts of the garden and then into the more relaxed and 'natural' areas such as the Pinetum and Lime Avenue. However, this should not deter the visitor from coming to this lovely and exciting place. Beyond the formal boundaries of the garden at Nymans lies several woodland walks, along with a Wild Garden and Rhododendron Wood, the latter both particularly beautiful in early spring and autumn.

**Getting there** National grid ref. TQ265294
- ◉ Handcross, near Haywards Heath, West Sussex, RH17 6EB.
- ◉ National Trust, tel 01444 405250, website: www.nationaltrust.org.uk
- ◉ On the B2114, nearest stations Balcombe four and a half miles (seven kilometres), Crawley five and a half miles (nine kilometres).
- ◉ **Other gardens nearby:** Borde Hill (see page 16).

# PARHAM

## STORRINGTON

I have lamented elsewhere in this book the unfortunate way that some houses and gardens have lost their original approach route and how as a consequence much of the initial drama and impact of arrival for the visitor is missing. Thankfully at Parham all is blissfully intact. First there is the reassuring gatehouse at the roadside, then the very long and sinuous drive through the beautiful park, complete with antlered deer and an exceedingly pretty dovecote, all culminating in the arrival at the beautiful 16th-century house. Backed by the Downs and surrounded on all sides by its own 120 hectares of parkland, Parham exudes an air of peace and stability that can only be created by generations of very careful stewardship.

The foundation stone of Parham house was laid by the two-year-old Thomas Palmer in 1577, and a changing cast of families has lived here ever since. It was the Pearson family who acquired Parham in 1922 and first opened house and garden to the public in the 1940s. A visit to the house reveals their careful restoration along with an impressive collection of furniture, paintings and textiles. Other longtime inhabitants are the aforementioned fallow deer, descendants of the original herd that dates back to 1628.

The garden is entered through the generous courtyard with central fountain, into the 18th-century Pleasure Grounds with a walk that follows the walls of the property and leads to an impressive set of iron gates, guarded by alert Istrian stone lions. Through the gateway lies the rectangular Walled Garden. Dating from the 1700s, it is intersected by paths, which effectively quarter the space (1.6 hectares). The whole perimeter is planted with abundant mixed borders and the walls are clothed in climbers and espaliered fruit trees. The main path is bounded by grass borders planted with hollies and behind these are rose-covered walls (note the stone herms at the end of the walls). The path terminates in a stone pavilion with walls decorated with an 18th-century marble cartouche complete with crest, *putti* and half skulls; a sobering momento mori amid all this vibrant abundance.

To the right of this path lies a greenhouse, Herb Garden, and large and expansive Vegetable and Cutting Garden. A little way along the path is a stone-edged doorway. This leads into a small potting area with neatly hung garden tools and paraphernalia. The wonderful scents that drift towards the visitor now lead you into one of the loveliest greenhouses I have yet seen. Long and narrow, it is formed from a wall on one side with a glassed roof and side constructed of teak. Ornate cast-iron benches topped with slate line the walls, although these are difficult to discern due to the numerous pots overflowing with a dazzling array of plants. The flowers of pelargonium, plumbago, fuchsia, datura and the stunning blue of morning glory all jostle against ivy and cactus. In the centre of the greenhouse wall a shallow segmental niche bows out and provides a seat with leaded lights set into the wall and a brick arch above. It is the quality of the design and craftsmanship that really sets this structure apart. Like all the other buildings in the Walled Garden it is the work of the Arts-and-Crafts-influenced architect Victor Heal and dates from the 1920s. Surprisingly Heal is now something of an obscure figure and his work under-acknowledged.

The path from the greenhouse leads into an area that has been sub-divided combining rich planting with grass and trees. Under a spreading cherry tree is a rather alarming sculpture of a classical male figure, apparently in the throes of dying (signed L. Armigoni, 1857). This area is bounded by one of the spans of the axial paths and planted on either side with a stunning gold theme. After it intersects in the centre the theme turns to a riot of blues and purples. Beyond the Gold Border is the Vegetable and Cutting Garden. Geometrically arranged beds are edged with high box hedges and contain an enticing mix of flowers, fruit and vegetables. Glamorous dark red cannas grow cheek by jowl with purple-sprouting and dusky calvo nero. Asparagus, corn, beans, leeks and squash all look quite as lovely as the dahlias with their array of bright and bold colours. Architectural clipped box cubes add formality and temper the overflowing herbaceous and mixed borders that edge the enclosing walls. Take care not to miss the Herb Garden which lies hidden within tall yew hedging, and has a circular brick pond. Note also the many semi-circular brick-built ponds and pumps that are studied throughout the Walled Garden, probably used as dipping pools for watering the garden originally.

Cross the main path and beyond an attractive rose-covered structure that spans a disused well and pump is the Lavender Garden. This unusual but very effective design consists of double rows of lavender planted in the lawn in the configuration of a cross with a large pot at the centre. The glaucous leaves of the lavender contrast well with the grass and the flowers are alive with bees and butterflies. Behind the Blue Border is the Orchard, the comparative simplicity of which contrasts well with the rest of this walled garden. Tucked into a corner near the Lavender Garden is the Wendy house, which under no circumstances should be missed! It was built for the three lucky daughters of the Hon. Clive Pearson. Stoop to enter and enjoy this Gulliver-like experience of a perfectly scaled-down version of a house complete with dresser, fireplace and wooden stairway to the first floor. Like the greenhouse, the standard of craftsmanship and attention to detail cannot be faulted.

As you leave the Walled Garden to the right is a fine three-arched summer house with a sculpture by Ivan Mestrovic. To the left is the impressive River God statue set against the wall and brought here in the mid-19th century by Robert Curzon. One of the particular features of the garden at Parham is the discreet and wholly appropriate placing of statuary and ornament, always adding to, rather than distracting from, its setting. Sloping down towards the Pleasure Pond is Veronica's Maze, an elaborate pattern cut into the grass and inset with brick. A relatively recent addition, installed in 1990 and named after Mrs Veronica Tritton, it is based on the embroidery covering the bed in the Great Chamber at Parham. The edge of the pond can be followed and provides a lovely gentle walk which leads to the classically styled Cannoch House overlooking the water. Note the birdsong and absence of traffic noise. Parham is one of the few gardens I have visited in Sussex that is mercifully insulated from the intrusive sound of the car.

**Getting there** National grid ref. TQ060142

- Parham Park Ltd., Storrington, near Pulborough, West Sussex, RH20 4HS.
- Parham Park Ltd., tel 01903 742021, website: www.parhaminsussex.co.uk
- On the A283 between Pulborough and Storrington, nearest station Pulborough, limited buses from Pulborough and Storrington.
- **Other gardens nearby:** Uppark, West Dean Gardens (see page 82).

# PETWORTH PARK

## PETWORTH

O ne of the joys of visiting many of the Sussex gardens featured in this book is the ideas and inspiration they provide. Endless hours of fun can be had deciding which particular features of a garden could be copied in one's own humble plot. Whether they are ever actually implemented or not is largely academic and need not mar the fantasy. However, few of us I think will visit the splendours of Petworth Park and seriously consider transposing many of its features into our own gardens. At 283 hectares, this is gardening on a truly monumental and grand scale.

Famous for its associations with the artist J.M.W. Turner and the landscape designer Lancelot 'Capability' Brown (*1716-83*), Petworth House is an exceptionally grand and imposing late 17th-century mansion (it is open to the public, although the park and grounds only can be visited). It is home to one of the finest collections of paintings, sculpture and furniture in Britain today. The landscape park in which it sits provides the visitor with an exemplary experience of the scale and style of garden that became so fashionable among the English aristocratic elite of the 18th century. The hallmarks of the style, as practised by Brown, include a gently rolling expanse of green parkland that runs right up to the house (protected from marauding cattle by a hidden ha-ha); large single specimens or groups and clumps of trees arranged to provide the best possible view and prospect; a more thickly wooded area at the perimeter edge of the property; all flanked by a wide sinuous drive at the boundary. A serpentine lake was also a prerequisite. The whole prospect, although completely contrived and man-made, is to appear as natural and harmonious as Nature would intend, that is, were she an artist!

The main innovator and populariser of the English landscape movement was 'Capability' Brown, and it is the mature realisation of his plan that we see at Petworth today. Previously there were much older formal gardens on the site, most notably a baroque design, probably by George London, dating from after the present house was built (*1688-93*). The Pleasure Ground at this time was of an Elizabethan design. It was the second Lord Egremont who employed Brown in 1751 and this resulted in a new design for the entire park being proposed the following year. From that point onwards Brown's work at Petworth is extremely well documented. Incredible though it may seem, it is vital to beware as you stroll around the grounds at Petworth that almost all you see is totally man-made and to gaze at the picture in the light of Michael Reed's assessment of Brown:

> *Using only three elements — trees, water and grass — he succeeded in creating an illusion of eternal tranquillity, something which, on a clear summer's day in the largest of his parks, as at Burghley or Petworth, it is still possible to recapture.*[1]

The beautiful serpentine lake to the west front of the house is perhaps the loveliest feature of the grounds at Petworth. Understandably it was a favourite subject for Turner during his frequent stays here during the 1820s. Some of his paintings of the Petworth lake can be seen in the house while many of the highly atmospheric gouaches he did of the interiors are at Tate Britain, London. By 1752, under Brown's direction, several small ponds had been transformed into this flat expanse of water by damming the stream which had originally fed them. This is known as the Upper Pond, while a Lower Pond can be found in the north-east corner of the park. To the right lies the ornate boat house. Also of

---

1. *Reed, Michael*, The Georgian Triumph 1700-1830, *Routledge & Kegan Paul, London, 1983, p99.*

interest is the large stone hound that stands on the pedestal in the shallow waters of the lake. It is by John Edward Carew (*1785-1868*) and portrays one of the third Earl's favourite hunting dogs, Alcibiacles, sadly said to have drowned at this spot. Wildfowl abound here and if the visitor is lucky the herd of fallow deer (the largest in Britain) that contentedly graze the park will put in an appearance. A turreted gothic folly can be seen in the distance on the ridge above the lake. This is probably the building simply described as the 'Tower for Lord Egremont' which Sir John Soane (*1753-1837*) designed in 1815. This whole scene would have been viewed from the house and appraised much as a landscape painting would have been.

On a walk through the gardens and park several carved stone urns mounted on pedestals will be found. These are of very high quality and are thought to have been commissioned by the second Earl from Robert Parsons, a sculptor from Bath, who also did work for Lord Burlington at Chiswick House. Several have been positioned in the island beds just to the north of the house and the beds are planted with box, bay, lavender, roses and mixed shrubs. Those interested in sculpture and garden ornament should take particular note of these areas immediately surrounding the house. The wrought-iron screens to the west front and the gates into the park were erected in 1872 and are copies of those at Hampton Court by Jean Tijou (*fl. c.1680s –1710s*). On the piers of the main gate, 17th-century carved trophies can now be seen. These were moved when Brown did away with the forecourt to the house and swept the park straight up to its walls. The trophies were reinstated in 1870 by the second Lord Leconfield (natural son of the third Lord Egremont).

The woodland area, to the north of the house, is known as the Pleasure Garden and was the area least altered by Brown. Here he introduced gravel serpentine paths, a ha-ha, a curved stone wall and augmented the existing planting with new trees and shrubs. Several of the sweet chestnuts, limes and plane trees seen here today date from Brown's time. Yet again, as with so many important and lovely Sussex gardens, Petworth suffered great losses during the 1987 storm. The Pleasure Garden alone lost a staggering 600 trees but has now been replanted. Just as in Brown's time, such planting is done with a vision for the enjoyment of future generations rather than our own.

The northern and southern extremes of the Pleasure Garden are marked by an Ionic rotunda (now roofless) and a Doric temple respectively; both buildings featured on Brown's 1752 plan. The rotunda was built in 1766 and gives far reaching views down to meadow and woods. The temple is thought to have been moved to its present position from elsewhere in the grounds by Brown. In it a memorial has been erected to Henry Scanwen Wyndham, who was killed in action at El Alamein in 1942, the words of which are worth some reflection.

> There be things the good of which and the use of which are beyond all calculation
> of worldly goods or earthly uses; things such as Love and Honour and the Soul of
> Man which cannot be bought with price and do not die with Death.

Sit here, ponder the memorial and enjoy the classic view down the parkland to the shelter belt of trees and shrubs and to the farmland beyond. The trees effectively obscure the road behind but do not, alas, obliterate the noise of the traffic, an unwelcome modern-day intrusion into this quintessential 18th-century idyll.

**Getting there** National grid ref. SU975219

- Petworth, West Sussex, GU28 0AE.
- National Trust, tel 01798 343929, website: www.nationaltrust.org.uk
- Buses to Petworth, nearest station Pulborough.
- **Other gardens nearby:** Denmans Gardens (see page 28), Parham (see page 64), Uppark, Walled Garden at Cowdray, Weald & Downland Museum, West Dean Gardens (see page 82).

# PRESTON PARK

## BRIGHTON

P reston Park was Brighton's first public park and is still its largest. It is an excellent example of a civic space that is used and enjoyed by locals and visitors 365 days a year. Whether it be dog walking, running, tennis, bowls, skate boarding, strolling, cycling, football, cricket, picnicking or simply enjoying a cup of tea at the Rotunda Café, this attractive 60-plus acre green open space accommodates all comers. During the Brighton Festival (May time) it is also home to great tented domes that house often exotic circus, theatre and dance performances.

The adjacent Preston Manor dates originally from the early 17th century but was rebuilt in 1738 with major additions made in the Edwardian period (for opening times, contact 01273 292770). Home to the Stanford family, what is now the park was originally the pleasure grounds of the Manor. During the early 1870s Mr Bennett-Stanford opened parts of his grounds to the public on Sundays then offered it for sale to Brighton Corporation in 1876 but the offer was declined. A generous bequest to the town in 1879 by local bookmaker William Edmund Davies of £70,000 provided the finances to purchase and develop the site and it was bought for £50,000 in 1883. After being fenced and landscaped Preston Park was formally opened to the public by the Mayor on 8 November of that year. When Ellen Thomas-Stanford died in 1928 the remaining grounds of the Manor, including the Walled Garden, were incorporated into the park, the railings removed and the grounds remodelled. During World War II much of the by then extensive park was turned into food-producing allotments as part of the Dig For Victory campaign.

The park is dissected by the London Road with Preston Manor and the majority of the land lying to the east while the Rock Garden is on the western side of the road. As the park is not fenced it can be accessed from all sides (although the Rock Garden and Walled Garden are locked at night). The main northern and southern approaches are marked with fine dolphin lamp standards (lacking their original lights and shades) from the 1920s and the dolphin motif is repeated in the stone balustrading.

One of the most prominent features of Preston Park is the brick, stone and terracotta Clock Tower. It is the work of Francis May and the foundation stone was laid by its benefactor Edward White in 1891 (the nearby Blaker's Park also boasts an impressive clock tower contemporaneously dating from 1893). A typically Victorian inscription preaches, 'Here I stand with all my might to tell the hour by day and night. Therefore example take by me and serve thy God as I serve thee.' Look closely beyond the surface coating of mindless graffiti on the fabric of the tower and yet more dolphin iconography is revealed, both in the decorative strap work relief panels and at the four corners as cherubic nereids ride on their dolphin mounts.

Since the 1950s the formal beds that run alongside the London Road have been planted out with elaborate bedding schemes as 'Gardens of Greeting.' The beds represent a Park Department from various towns around the country and each competes to produce the best design. Latterly a Peace Flower bed has also been added. It is this part of the park, known as The Gallops, which saw the loss of several massive trees in the 1987 storm. In 1953 the Garden for the Blind was created; it sits just below the lawns of Preston Manor to the north. Designed by the then Superintendent of Parks and Gardens, J.R.B. Evison, it was presented as a gift to the people of the town by Brighton Corporation and by the Butchers of Brighton, Hove and Portslade to commemorate the coronation of Elizabeth II. The Soroptimist Club provided the guide rails that circumnavigate the area, the Auctioneers Association and various locals contributed to other amenities, while the local branch of the Round Table provided, appropriately enough, the round table on the lawn. The dovecote was a present from the Mayor and originally housed Barbary doves to 'coo at the people using the garden.' The once attractive Arts and Crafts-style shelter is now a rather sad graffiti-covered tumbled down version of its former self and when I last visited was far from sweet smelling!

Opened again after extensive restoration in 2001 the Edwardian Walled Garden is a fine example of its type. Accessed both from the Garden for the Blind and from the grounds of Preston Manor the space is divided by paths laid on a north-south and east-west axis, at the centre of which sits a sundial. Period varieties of plants have been used to create a very successful combination of herbaceous planting. Cistus, peonies, foxgloves, poppies, roses, nigella, geraniums and roses; all the old favourites are here. A note of formality has been introduced with apple trees cordoned diagonally against the north wall and an iron tunnel covered in purple clematis. At the foot of the south-western wall is the pets' cemetery. Ellen Thomas-Stanford's favoured dogs rest here (their portraits in oil still hang on the walls of the Manor) along with many other canine and feline inhabitants including one of the erstwhile Royal Pavilion cats.

Towards the southern end of the park a grand wide brick path intersects the lawns and gradually rises through a series of shallow steps and terminates in a cool, classically inspired bowls pavilion. Another much more rustic pavilion lies to the south set amongst the immaculate bowling greens. The players, smartly dressed in their whites, present a tranquil and lovely sight throughout the playing season. Ample seats are provided for spectators and fragrant roses scramble up pillars.

At the southern tip of the park are the Rotunda Café and the Rose Garden. The Rotunda is a charming example of a 1920s and 1930s tea pavilion influenced by the principles of the Modernist movement. The building sits on a raised platform overlooking a formal design of water and stone across to the Rose Garden beyond, creating an interesting interplay of inside and outside spaces. A beautiful bronze lion head spouts water accompanied by two smaller fish-head spouts. The Rose Garden has been completely replanted with David Austin English Roses. These have been densely planted and grow with obvious vigour and health. The perimeter beds are filled with shrubs, bulbs and herbaceous planting, while the yew hedges behind are recovering after renovation and will provide a fitting shelter to the garden. Statues, urns and vases act as focal points set among the roses. However, one questions the decision to paint the statues black and gold when weathered stone would have endured so much better.

Cross the busy London Road to the north and you enter the Rock Garden, originally known as The Rookery. Constructed from 1,350 tonnes of Cheddar stone, it is said to be based on the design of the Chinese Willow Pattern. A beautifully constructed rugged stone path (though only for the sure-footed!) climbs up to the wisteria-clad wooden bridge which provides a view to the large pond below. In summer this is thick with water lilies and giant gunnera. Huge stepping stones provide another bridge across the water. If the prospect of the climb daunts, then there is still much to enjoy at ground level. Sit by the pond and watch the fish or explore the pretty pavilion, though sadly the surrounding landscaping is in need of renovation. The area is planted sympathetically, with acers and conifers contributing much to the oriental atmosphere, the roar of the continual traffic the only thing to remind you you have not stepped into the scene made familiar by so many blue-and-white china plates.

It could be said that Preston Park is a civic green space dressed up as an English landscape park. It is much more a park of trees and rolling lawns than of flower beds and floral clocks. The architecture of its buildings and features is of a quality not usually found in municipal areas. At a time when so many public parks are becoming increasingly neglected, the people of Brighton and Hove should applaud their city parks department for continuing to maintain Preston Park in such good heart.

**Getting there**                                    National grid ref. TQ305061
❯ London Road, Brighton, East Sussex.
❯ Brighton & Hove City Council, tel 01273 290000, website: www.brighton-hove.gov.uk
❯ Frequent buses from Brighton city centre, nearest stations Preston Park and London Road.
❯ **Other gardens nearby:** Pavilion Gardens, Kipling Gardens (see page 43).

# STANDEN

## EAST GRINSTEAD

Standen was built between 1892 and 1894 by the Arts and Crafts architect Philip Webb (*1831-1915*) as a country home for a London solicitor, James Beale, his wife Margaret and their large family. Built on the site of an existing farm, Webb incorporated the original farmhouse into his design, linking it with an archway to the new house. In true Arts and Crafts spirit, this substantial house presents a richly varied and asymmetrical façade and skyline.

All the principal views from the house are from the rear, which has a southerly aspect over the garden, Medway Valley and Ashdown Forest. The South Lawn is terminated by a ha-ha, so the garden appears to melt into the surrounding countryside without any boundary. On this elevation is the extensive conservatory which leads out onto the wide and expansive gravelled terrace. Interestingly a different position for the house was originally chosen by the landscape gardener G.B. Simpson, who also produced a garden plan, long before Webb was appointed as architect. Once on board Webb repositioned the house as he wished the new building to sit in harmony with the existing vernacular farmstead. Standen reflects the Arts and Crafts movement's ethos of using building materials that are common to the local area: stone quarried on site, Horsham brick, Wealden hung tiles and weather-boarding.

Simpson's original plan for the 5-hectare site was in the rather fussy Victorian gardenesque style, an aesthetic that was at odds with Webb's more naturalistic approach. Something of this tension between the two plans remains in the garden structure and has never been totally resolved. Added to this was the owner's own enthusiasm for design and planting and many changes continued to be made at Mrs Beale's request until well into the 1920s. Once the Trust gained the property in 1972 the planting of the garden was rationalised and a more complementary balance between design and generous planting has now been achieved. The Trust enthusiastically continues its ongoing plan of garden restoration, aiming to show the garden more in the spirit that Webb might have wished and one which reflects the principles of garden making that William Morris set out in his 1879 lecture 'Making the Best of It',

> large and small, it should look both orderly and rich. It should be well fenced
> from the outside world. It should by no means imitate either the wilfulness or
> wildness of nature, but should look like a thing never to be seen except near a
> house. It should in fact look like part of the house.

The garden at Standen is littered with enticing places to sit which accommodate all weathers, a particular favourite is the covered area next to the conservatory. Here the walls are lined with beautiful blue and white Delft tiles. Webb is quoted as commenting, 'there is no bad weather, only different kinds of weather' and the liberal smattering of covered seating areas at Standen rather reflect this thinking. Of necessity the garden incorporates several flights of steps, descending lawns and banks, due to the sloping nature of the site. Webb's terrace, steps and the lovely summerhouses that are used to terminate long vistas, are all typical of gardens in the Arts and Crafts style. The summer house on the Top Terrace was added in 1910. It was built to align with the spire of West Hoathly Church which, due to mature trees, is no longer visible. Naturalised spring bulbs grace the nearby lawns early in the year.

The former quarry has been transformed into an intriguing sunken garden. Narrow steep steps descend deeply into a cool, dank, fern-covered interior, complete with small pool inhabited by goldfish. The Quarry Garden is overhung with rhododendrons, camellias and acers. The sound of trickling water adds to the slightly gothic and melancholy air. Once out of the quarry and into the sunlight a wander through the garden reveals an interesting and varied range of mature trees.

The Bamboo Garden has undergone extensive restoration. Originally the site of an old rose garden much of the rampant bamboo has been cleared. During restoration the old swimming pool, used by the Beale children in long-gone summers, was rediscovered. This has now been reinstated, complete with cascade. The Bamboo garden leads into the Orchard contained by high hedges. Elevated above this is the Croquet Lawn with views across the orchard to the countryside beyond.

The house originally had a large hedged kitchen garden with extensive glasshouses. Here produce was grown both for the Beales' London home and for Standen. The Kitchen Garden today is smaller than the original and in more recent years had been planted as a rose garden but has now been returned to its former purpose. Generous rectangular beds are punctuated with upright yew trees which form an avenue down the centre of the gently sloping garden. Pear trees occupy the centre of the beds while wonderful old knarled espaliered apples, dating from 1891, frame the edge of the garden. The long-term aim of the Trust is to grow the type of vegetables, fruit, herbs and flowers that would have flourished here in the Beales' time.

The interior of the house is furnished with Arts and Crafts wallpapers, textiles, carpets, furniture and ceramics, many by Morris & Co., presenting a complete view of a house of this period and style and a visit is much recommended. However, it is also possible to visit the garden alone and there are several sign-posted woodland walks that can be enjoyed from the property.

---

**Getting there**                                    National grid ref. TQ387353

❯ West Hoathly Road, East Grinstead, West Sussex, RH19 4NE.

❯ National Trust, tel 01342 323029, website: www.nationaltrust.org.uk

❯ Two miles (three kilometres) south of East Grinstead, signposted from the B2110.
Bus from East Grinstead to Saint Hill then half mile (one kilometre) walk along footpath.
Two miles (three kilometres) from East Grinstead Station.

❯ **Other gardens nearby:** Borde Hill (see page 16), Nymans Garden (see page 59),
Sheffield Park, Wakehurst Place.

# SYLVIA STANDING GARDEN

## HORSHAM

Unlike so many of the large and expansive gardens made by the great and the good, this pearl of a garden is small and modest, created entirely by enthusiastic and generous volunteers. Quite understandably the gardens that tend to be on the usual visitor trail are those with the most high-profile historical connections, the most impressive or specialist collection plants or indeed simply the largest advertising budget. Inevitably a handful of my selections for this book perhaps fall prey to some of these traits but they are also jolly good gardens to see. However, this modest delight hidden in the centre of Horsham is in no way guilty of any such boasts and is all the more worthy of a visit for just that reason.

The Sylvia Standing Garden lies tucked behind Horsham Museum in the heart of this busy market town. Causeway House, now Horsham Museum, is a wonderful 15th-century building with some later additions. It stands in an oasis of calm called The Causeway – an ancient area of Horsham hidden behind the 19th-century town hall. For many years the area that now flourishes as a garden had been subject to years of neglect and decay. What lay here were weeds, the rotting remains of a former summerhouse and conservatory, along with overgrown shrubs, all intertwined with an impenetrable trail of bindweed and ground elder. To the rescue came the visionary local figure Sylvia Standing who saw potential in this sad site. With the enthusiastic and energetic help of members of the Horsham Museum Society, Sylvia and her team set about clearing the site in 1981. This was an ambitious and daunting task with the only plant material worth salvaging a wisteria and a chaenomeles.

The structure of the garden was established using an interesting and very attractive mix of stone that has been recycled from local archaeological digs. Sussex marble, Roman mosaic, locally produced bricks and Tudor iron slag all contribute to the eclectic palette. The layout is formal, which suits the intimacy of this enclosed walled garden and makes the best use of the limited space. The central focal point being provided by a traditional sundial. As befits its museum setting, the garden is home to a collection of diverse objects including a lead pump, two local milestones, two parish boundary stones, a bronze sculpture of fighting birds by J.G. Millais, a cauldron and some old stone sinks. However, this miscellany of objects is discreetly arranged within the area and certainly lends nothing of the air of the car boot or jumble sale to the garden. The central beds are planted with fragrant herbs, designed to give particular pleasure to the visually impaired. The ample walls are clothed with climbers. A remarkable variety of plants are grown for such a relatively small area and a helpful and informative planting list is available which well illustrates just how many varieties of plants can be grown in a relatively compact space. Old favourites such as rose, clematis, vine and Japanese quince clothe the surrounding walls and shelter numerous bulbs, perennials and herbs.

Initially the restoration of the garden was funded by Horsham Museum Society and its maintenance paid for by the sale of plants and seeds. The museum now funds it (and I'm sure donations from appreciative visitors are always welcome). Sylvia Standing worked at the garden until her retirement in 2003 since when an active team of volunteers has continued her sterling work. The garden is testament to what can be achieved when the vision and commitment of local people is backed by a helpful District Council. I hope it will prove an inspiration to all who visit and may even open our eyes to new possibilities for those disused and abandoned places in our own local environments. Without action these spaces simply fester and deteriorate further.

Due to its modest size, a visit to this garden will afford you time for other pleasures. Certainly the main museum collection warrants a look. As well as the main building there is a very interesting rural collection in the barn beyond the garden. Note the 1900 Green of Leeds lawnmower that still looks like it could make short shrift of most domestic lawns over 100 years after its manufacture. The Sussex shepherd's smocks are also very beautiful (if unrelated to gardening!) Within easy driving distance is Architectural Plants at Nuthurst, the plant nursery par excellence, where you can stock up on the unusual, exotic or the just plain large.

**Getting there**                                    National grid ref. TQ170304

- 9 The Causeway, Horsham, West Sussex, RH12 1HE.
- Horsham District Council, tel 01403 254959, website: www.horshammuseum.org
- Nearest station Horsham, good bus service.
- **Other gardens nearby:** Leonardslee (see page 46), Nymans Gardens (see page 59).

# WEST DEAN GARDENS

## CHICHESTER

West Dean Gardens provide a good example of a site which has a long and distinguished history yet has been able to adapt to the changing world around it with great success and considerable style. The original West Dean manor house dated back to 1622 but it was the second Lord Selsey in 1804 who rebuilt the impressive house which now sits at the centre of the estate, designed by the architect James Wyatt (*1746-1813*). The Orangery also dates from this period. Caroline Harcourt, sister of the third Lord, inherited the estate in 1835 on the death of her brother. During her stewardship she was instrumental in substantially developing the landscape and also began the arboretum. At her death the 2,430-hectare estate went out of the family and was eventually bought by the wealthy William Dodge James.

During the late Victorian and Edwardian eras James, along with his successful hostess wife Evie, ensured that West Dean provided the perfect welcome to a demanding country house set that included the Prince of Wales and King Alphonso of Spain. Fashionable architect Ernest George advised on remodelling the house while his partner, Harold Peto, improved the gardens and grounds. William James died in 1912 and as his son Edward was still a minor, the house was let to a series of tenants, resulting in the gardens being subjected to gradual neglect and decline. It was not until 1932 that Edward came into his inheritance aged 25 and the house and grounds reverted to him.

Edward James (*1907-84*) was an avid supporter of the Surrealist movement, an art collector and a poet. He spent much of his life abroad in California and Mexico, making only occasional visits to West Dean. When there he usually stayed at the Lutyens-designed house Monkton, which his father had built on a high point of the estate and which James remodelled and characteristically filled with Surrealist excess. Wishing to find a useful and productive role for his inherited English country estate, James founded a charitable trust, The Edward James Foundation, in 1964. Its aim was, and remains, to encourage music, visual arts and the practice of traditional crafts. Fortunately the trust has also ensured the continuing protection and prosperity of house, gardens and grounds. West Dean College now occupies the house and offers a lively and stimulating programme of courses.

The gardens provide a varied range of experiences including the walled kitchen gardens and greenhouses, the park and St Roche's Arboretum. Devastating damage caused by the storm of 1987 was greeted as an opportunity to re-evaluate the site and take a bold new approach to the future of the garden. The Visitor Centre, built in a somewhat fussy version of the local vernacular, opened in 1996 and was part of these new developments.

The beautifully restored complex of walled kitchen and fruit gardens is one of the most impressive in the country and makes a visit to West Dean an absolute must for all vegetable growers. The gardens were established in their present position during the 1804 redevelopment of the house and the tall enclosing walls were also erected at this time. William James rebuilt and extended many of the glasshouses. During their Edwardian heyday the kitchen and fruit gardens would have kept more than half the workforce of the whole garden (11 men) busy. Post 1987 this area underwent an enthusiastic and extensive regeneration and now produces a tempting range of fruit and vegetables.

The Fruit Garden benefits from a 'crinkle-crankle' wall, *c.*1810. Such walls were usually serpentine in shape, each bay on the southern side of the wall providing a sheltered microclimate for precious plants. The West Dean wall is unusual as it is angular rather than sinuous but the principle is the same. Over 200 varieties of apples, pears, plums and cherries are grown in a range of ways including as half-standard trees, espaliers and cordons in a bewildering array of shapes. The magical circular thatched building set into the garden walls was built as an apple store and still has the racks inside awaiting the autumn's harvest. An iron pergola acts as support to a large variety of roses with generously planted herbaceous borders in front. Here you can glimpse busy bees at work foraging back and forth from garden to hive.

From near total dereliction the 13 glasshouses, three cold frames and a hot-bed have been lovingly restored to a very high standard and are one of the highlights of a visit here. They primarily date from the last decade of the 19th century. The 13 houses have been divided in such a way as to provide 26 different environments, each providing optimum growing conditions for various types of plants. Figs, grapes, peaches, strawberries, peppers, tomatoes, aubergines, melons, cucumbers, flowers, ferns and unusual and decorative gourds can all be seen thriving in the immaculately kept glasshouses during the season. Chilli peppers have also become a firm favourite with the gardeners at West Dean and a beguiling variety is grown here. Indeed such is the enthusiasm for the hot and spicy that a Chilli Festival is held at the gardens annually, as are similar events devoted to tomatoes and apples.

The array of vegetables grown in the outdoor kitchen garden is quite as enticing as those found within the cosy confines of the glasshouses and offers much visual as well as culinary delight. On my last visit a box-edged bed had been planted with a rich pattern of herbs and vegetables, including bronze and lime green lettuces, arranged in a traditional knot pattern. Sweet peas scrambled up obelisks to lend some vertical interest. The Visitor Centre restaurant uses some of the abundant produce, the cut flowers grace the college and the fruit is on sale to the public.

One of the delights of the gardens, and perhaps its most important historical feature, is the stone and flint pergola that crosses the North Lawn behind the house. The impressive 100-metre long pergola was designed by Peto and completed just prior to William's death. The young Edward James laid the foundation stone. The classically-inspired pergola is constructed of 62 columns, each supporting varieties of rose, wisteria, honeysuckle or clematis. A formal sunken pool marks the centre. To the west the pergola terminates in a charming gazebo, the exterior finely patterned in a chequer-board of flint and stone panels. A modern engraved window illustrates some of the arts and crafts practised at the college. The gazebo boasts an unusual floor of knapped flints and equine molars! A small amphitheatre towards the opposite end of the pergola plays host to numerous open-air performances in summer. The Sunken Garden at the eastern end may also be by Peto. Alongside the pergola a former tennis court now serves as a much-used bowling green, over-looked by a rustic summerhouse, formerly used as an aviary. A similar summerhouse can be found by the Sunken Garden, and both of them date from the 19th century.

The parkland stretches out from the house and contains a multitude of beautiful mature trees, including several Cedars of Lebanon. The Cedar of Lebanon is thought to be the first ornamental tree introduced into Britain in the 17th century. Towards the North Lawn is a specimen that is believed to have been planted *c.*1748, and so is probably one of the oldest in Sussex.

The house at West Dean presents a grand façade. Clipped geometric yews frame the entrance and the theme is continued around the house. To the west of the house is a long terrace with formal flower beds laid out to the original Victorian design and a tall yew hedge with crenellated top. The River Lavant meanders through the Spring and Wild Gardens and is crossed by rustic stone and flint bridges. To the front of the house the river provides a natural ha-ha allowing the lawn to seamlessly stretch into the grazed parkland beyond. The Spring Garden has been restored to some of its former glory, the laburnum tunnel reinstated and the planting given an exotic touch with the introduction of feature plants such as tree ferns and bamboos. Beyond lies the Wild Garden with views to the parkland glimpsed through an interesting collection of trees.

An enjoyable hour's circular walk can be taken through the parkland which leads to the 20-hectare St Roche's Arboretum. Originally dating back to the 1830s and 1840s, an enthusiastic programme of planting has continued to the present day. A large variety of trees thrive including natives, exotics and the large Himalayan rhododendrons introduced by William James. Sheltered within a glade here lies Edward James's grave, a simple slab of Cumbrian slate inscribed by John Skelton. Two female coade-stone statues lend a suitably melancholy air. Do stop for a moment and pay tribute to the man whose far-sighted generosity has allowed West Dean College and Gardens to continue to blossom and thrive.

**Getting there**                                 National grid ref. SU864126
- West Dean, Chichester, West Sussex, PO18 0QZ.
- The Edward James Foundation, tel 01243 811301, website: www.westdean.org.uk
- Six miles (10 kilometres) north of Chichester on the A286. Nearest station Chichester.
- **Other gardens nearby:** Denmans Gardens (see page 28), Petworth (see page 68), Uppark, The Walled Garden at Cowdray, Weald & Downland Museum.

# GLOSSARY

**Lancelot 'Capability' Brown (1716-83)** Brown was the leading figure of the English landscape movement which aimed to arrange parkland, water and woodland in a seemingly 'natural' way. He undertook a huge number of commissions, was extremely influential and is considered to have been the first professional landscape designer.

**Carpet bedding** A very popular style of flower bed with the Victorians, who had the man-power, time and money to implement it on often quite a large scale. Elaborate patterns were created using numerous low-growing flowers and plants. Great care was needed to ensure that the plant material used was of a similar habit so no one plant dominated with superior height or speed of growth. Foliage plants, particularly succulents such as house leeks, were initially favoured and gave the tightest design, although flowers were introduced over time. The skill and maintenance involved make such beds impractical for most domestic gardens but they were very popular in municipal parks, although less so in recent years due to diminishing numbers of gardeners and to changing tastes.

**Coade stone** This 'stone' was widely used to make garden ornaments of all kinds; urns, statues, fountains etc. between 1769 and 1843. It looks like natural limestone but is actually an artificial ceramic and ornaments in prolific numbers were produced by Mrs Eleanor Coade in her London factory.

**Cordon** A fruit tree trained to grow as a single straight stem.

**Crinkle-crankle wall**  A wall constructed as a serpentine curve, usually south-facing, in which the individual bays form sheltered microclimates for the cultivation of tender plants.

**Doric**  One of the orders of classical architecture which describes the form and decoration of the column and entablature (the horizontal block supported by the columns below). Doric columns are the plainest of the orders and are characterised by no decoration on the capital (the top of the column) and has a plain or fluted shaft (the main trunk of the column).

**Espalier**  A technique for training fruit trees flat against a wall or along a freestanding support of wires.

**Eyecatcher**  In a landscape park an eyecatcher is a feature, such as a monument, building or tower, placed at some distance and usually on a high point. However, in a smaller-scale setting a large tree, shrub or piece of garden ornament could be deployed as an eyecatcher to focus the attention of the viewer.

**Gardenesque**  This term describes a Victorian preference for planting and arranging plants in such a way that the individual characteristics of each plant are seen to their best advantage. It was first coined by the garden writer and designer J.C. Loudon in 1832.

**Gazebo**  A small garden building or shelter positioned to afford attractive views across the garden.

**Ha-ha**  A deep ditch used to contain and restrict the movement of livestock. Ha-has are used to create a sense of endless, unfenced rolling country and were particularly popular in large landscape parks.

**Herm**  A rectangular, often tapering pedestal topped by a head. Used in decorative stonework.

**Hot-bed**  A growing bed which has been filled with fermenting material such as manure which both feeds and heats plants creating ideal forcing conditions. Often covered with a glass frame.

**Ionic**  One of the orders of classical architecture which describes the form and decoration of the column and entablature (the horizontal block supported by the columns below). Ionic columns are characterised by curled volutes on the capital (the top of the column) and a fluted shaft (the main trunk of the column).

**Island bed** A flower or shrub bed, often circular, cut into an area of open grass or lawn.

**Christopher Lloyd (1921-2006)** One of the most popular and respected garden writers of the late 20th century. His long-running column for the magazine *Country Life* was a firm favourite. He developed the highly influential garden at Great Dixter and was an accomplished plantsman.

**Loggia** A covered area, often of considerable length and open at the sides. It can be attached on one side to a building.

**Sir Edwin Lutyens (1869-1944)** Arts and Crafts architect who, often in collaboration with Gertrude Jekyll, designed many influential gardens at home and abroad. Both Lutyens and Jekyll closely linked their gardens to the architectural context of the house, using the same palette of building materials for garden structures.

**Pavilion** A term used for a garden building which originally referred to a canvas tent but that grew over time to encompass such grand structures as the Royal Pavilion at Brighton! Mostly it refers to more modest structures that can either be open to the garden or enclosed by doors.

**Pergola** A structure consisting of uprights and connecting joists or arches, usually repeated to create a tunnel-like effect. The uprights act as supports for climbing plants.

**Harold Peto (1854-1933)** Peto began life as an architect but changed to interior and garden design. Until 1892 he worked in a successful partnership with Ernest George. His garden designs are deeply influenced by detailed study of Italian gardens, coupled with an appreciation of the individual site. His own garden, Iford Manor, is a wonderful example of his ethos and can be seen near Bradford-on-Avon, in Wiltshire.

**Picturesque** An 18th-century movement most often associated with Richard Payne Knight and Sir Uvedale Price. Features particularly associated with landscape painting, notably wild, irregular and dramatic scenery, were incorporated into large gardens, augmented by contrasting foliage and 'wild,' unkempt trees and shrubs; rather the antithesis of Brown's manicured parkland landscapes. Humphry Repton favoured his own scaled-down version of the picturesque which included flower gardens.

**Pleaching**  Conjure up a mental picture of a hedge on stilts and there you have a row of pleached trees. The branches of a line of trees, often limes, are intertwined and trimmed to create the effect of a hedge in the air.

**Potager**  A kitchen or vegetable and fruit garden usually arranged for some ornamental, as well as functional, effect.

**James Pulham junior  (c.1820-98)**
The 'Son' part of James Pulham and Son who were leading landscape gardeners in the 19th and early 20th centuries. Large and impressive rockeries were their speciality, they produced those at Buckingham Palace and the Royal Horticultural Society Gardens at Wisley. They used natural stone often in combination with a very convincing copy which they constructed from rubble covered with cement which became known as Pulhamite.

**Humphry Repton (1752-1818)**
Repton was the next big name on the landscape design scene after Brown. He continued many of Brown's ideas concerning the design of parkland but also incorporated flower beds near the house, these were sometimes quite formal in design. Part of his legacy is the wonderful series of Red

Books which were prepared for clients. Each contains a series of watercolours which show the garden both before and (once the flap is lifted) after the proposed improvements.

**Rill**  Sometimes a small stream or brook but in formal gardens usually a sunken channel filled with water for decorative effect.

**Rotunda**  A circular building often constructed of columns supporting a domed roof. Can be open or enclosed.

**Stumpery**  Stumperies were a popular feature in Victorian gardens. They were made from tree roots and stumps, often arranged upside down and adorned with trailing ivies etc. to create a general air of gothic gloom.

# OTHER GARDENS
# TO VISIT IN SUSSEX

**Arundel Castle,**
**Arundel, West Sussex**
*Telephone 01903 882173*
*www.arundelcastle.org*
Over 16 hectares of beautiful
grounds and a series of stunning
gardens that include walled kitchen
and flower gardens with Victorian
glasshouses growing exotic fruit
and vegetables in a great setting.

**Herstmonceux Castle,**
**Hailsham, East Sussex**
*Telephone 01323 833816*
*www.herstmonceux-castle.com*
Lovely Elizabethan-style gardens
and parkland surround this 15th-
century moated castle, originally
built as a country home. The
walled garden dates from 1570.
Other delights include an ancient
sweet chestnut avenue, herb
garden, the Shakespeare Garden,
a folly, woodland sculptures and,
weather permitting, a waterfall.

**High Beeches Gardens,**
**Handcross, West Sussex**
*Telephone 01444 400589*
*www.highbeeches.com*
A garden of contrasts made of 10
hectares of enchanting woodland,
meadow and water gardens. From
spring to autumn each season
presents something new. Daffodils,
bluebells, orchids, cowslips,
magnolias and azaleas all thrive
in abundance here and the willow
gentians are of particular note.

**Lamb House, Rye, East Sussex**
*Telephone 01580 762334*
*www.nationaltrust.org.uk*
This fine Georgian house and
walled garden was formally the
home of the very differing novelists
Henry James and later E.F. Benson.
Both house and garden were
used as the setting for many of the
latter's Mapp and Lucia comic
novels. The picturesque streets

of Rye were lightly disguised as the fictional town of Tilling. Though relatively small, the garden pretty and well worth a visit; it has one of the most delightful, if poignant, pets' cemeteries.

## Pavilion Gardens, Brighton, East Sussex

*Telephone 0300 029 0900*
*www.royalpavilion.org.uk*
After extensive restoration in the mid-1980s the Royal Pavilion Gardens can now be seen in all their authentic Regency splendour. The survival of the original planting lists proved invaluable during the recreation of the gardens and many of the plants seen today are early 19th-century cultivars and introductions. Serpentine paths and profusely blooming island beds create a colourful, and appropriate, setting for the ornamental excesses of the Pavilion beyond.

## Pashley Manor, Ticehurst, East Sussex

*Telephone 01580 200888*
*www.pashleymanorgardens.com*
A beautifully maintained garden in the quintessential English Country House style which displays several historical periods. Pashley Manor is set within a delightful rural location with impressive views.

## Sheffield Park, near Uckfield, East Sussex

*Telephone 01825 790231*
*www.nationaltrust.org.uk*
Stunning 18th-century landscape garden of 48 hectares, designed by 'Capability' Brown, which has everything: mature trees, shrubs, lakes which provide spring, summer and autumn colour. Its later owner, Arthur G. Soames, added much to the garden in the early 20th century. Well worth a visit throughout the year.

## Southover Grange, Lewes, East Sussex

*Telephone 01273 484999*
*www.lewes.gov.uk*
This walled park is the garden to Southover Grange (not open to the public). The Elizabethan house was once home to the horticulturalist and diarist John Evelyn (1620-1706) and later to the harpsicord player Violet Gordon Woodhouse. A romantic collection of semi-ruined walls and archways assembled from the Caen stone of the old Southover Priory (a casualty of the dissolution of the monasteries) forms the focal point of the grounds. There is a fine herbaceous border and intricate formal bedding-out schemes planted alongside the Winterbourne stream. The 350-year old mulberry tree is one of the oldest in the country.

**Uppark,**
**South Harting, West Sussex**
*Telephone 01730 825415*
*www.nationaltrust.org.uk*
Uppark suffered a devastating fire in 1989 and has since undergone a transforming programme of restoration. The grounds, originally designed by Humphry Repton, have also been subject to an extensive scheme of restoration and now much more faithfully reflect their early 19th-century picturesque influences.

**Walled Garden at Cowdray,**
**Midhurst, West Sussex**
*Telephone 01730 816881*
*www.walledgardencowdray.co.uk*
An imaginative and sensitive restoration of the historic Walled Garden at Cowdray begun in 2001, which sits alongside the ruins of a Tudor mansion. Laid out using a traditional geometric medieval design, the beds overflow with scented flowers, roses, herbs and vegetables.

**Wakehurst Place,**
**near Ardingly, West Sussex**
*Telephone 01444 894066*
*www.kew.org*
Wakehurst is Kew Garden's country estate and as one might expect displays one of the world's most interesting collection of plants. It is also home to the national collections of betula, hypericum, nothofagus and skimmia. A whole day can easily be filled in its 69 hecares, quite apart from the Millenium Seed Bank exhibition. A must for any garden visitor to Sussex.

**Weald and Downland Open Air**
**Museum, Singleton, West Sussex**
*Telephone 01243 811363*
*www.wealddown.co.uk*
Experience seven authentic period buildings, ranging from a 13th-century flint cottage to a pair of timber-framed early Victorian labourer's cottages, all with their historically correct accompanying gardens.

**Wellingham Herb Garden,**
**near Ringmer, East Sussex**
*Telephone 01435 883187*
A treasure of a small, little-known walled herb garden dating from 1818 which has undergone extensive restoration since 1992. Yew and box provide formal hedging for herb-filled beds while roses and fruit, including medlars, clothe the walls. An early 19th-century gazebo overlooks the garden from the neighbouring property.

# INDEX